DIVING

the

Virgin Islands

Hunter Publishing, Inc.
300 Raritan Center Parkway
Edison NJ 08818
Tel (908) 225 1900
Fax (908) 417 0482

ISBN 1-55650-700-3

© 1996 Lynn Seldon Jr.

Cover Photo: *Diver and Elkhorn coral in the British Virgin Islands* by Jim Scheiner, Rainbow Visions, Tortola

DIVING

the

Virgin Islands

Lynn Seldon Jr.

Acknowledgements

No book of this scope could have been written without help from a variety of sources. I employed the buddy system to make this the best possible dive travel guide to the Virgin Islands and wish to thank many people.

The British Virgin Islands Tourist Board and the United States Virgin Islands Government Tourist Offices were big assets for me from the time I started research for this book. They can also be of help to future visitors, offering a wide range of printed material and advice.

A number of public relations firms and people, including FCB/Leber Katz, Barker Campbell & Farley, Development Counsellors International, Robinson, Yesawich, & Pepperdine, Scott Jones and Beth Hanssen at PADI, Ahrlene Stevens in the USVI, and many others were also helpful way beyond the normal call of duty. Sean Combs, editor of *Dive Training* magazine, has also been instrumental in helping me (and my column's readers) explore dive travel in the Virgin Islands and other locales.

For getting to the Virgin Islands, I can highly recommend American Airlines, Continental, and USAir. I have lots of personal experience (and frequent flier miles) with these airlines and they offer many convenient connections between the U.S. and the Virgin Islands.

I received a warm welcome everywhere I went in the Virgin Islands, but many people and places deserve specific thanks.

In the British Virgin Islands, a wide variety of resorts and restaurants welcomed me with typically British and Caribbean charm. My BVI hosts included: Long Bay Beach Resort & Villas; The Moorings; Biras Creek Estate; Bitter End Yacht Club & Resort; Little Dix Bay; Olde Yard Inn; Drake's Anchorage; and Peter Island. Dive operators who helped with the research for this book include Baskin in the Sun, Dive B.V.I., and Rainbow Visions Photography.

On St. Croix: Elizabeth Armstrong at The Buccaneer Hotel; the late Betty Sperper and her family at the King Christian Hotel; Kevin and Suzanne Ryan at the Waves at Cane Bay; and the staff of Anchor Inn, Carambola Beach Resort, Caravelle Hotel, and Villa Madeleine. Great food, drink, and company were found at the Aqua-Lounge Club, The Buccaneer, Café Madeleine; Kendrick's; and Top Hat. Dive operators who were particularly helpful include Anchor Dive Center, Dive St. Croix, and The Waves at Cane Bay, but all of the current operators on the island supported this project above and below the surface.

On St. John: The staff at Caneel Bay, Gallows Point, Hyatt Regency St. John, and Raintree Inn. Memorable meals were had at Le Château Bordeaux, Lucy's Bar & Restaurant, Ellington's, Etta's, The Fish Trap, The Lime Inn, and Pusser's. Dive operators who were eager to assist include Cruz Bay Watersports, Low Key Watersports, and Paradise Watersports, but all operators on St. John are perfect partners for a dive vacation.

On St. Thomas: Dick and Joyce Doumeng at Bolongo; the staff at Admiral's Inn, Bluebeard's Castle, Marriott's Frenchman's Reef, Grand Palazzo, Hotel 1829, Point Pleasant, Ramada Yacht Haven Hotel & Marina, Sapphire Beach, and Stouffer Grand Beach. I had delicious meals at Agave Terrace, Entre Nous, Eunice's Terrace, For the Birds, Hard Rock Café, Hotel 1829, Victor's New Hideout, and many more. Dive operators that deserve a special mention include Billy Bad Watersports, Chris Sawyer, and Dive In.

This book would not have been possible without the support of Kim André at Hunter Publishing, who believes scuba diving should be a major part of any vacation experience in the Virgin Islands.

My favorite buddy above and below the surface is my wife, Cele. Through this project, we both developed an immense love for everything in the Virgin Islands. I hope this book leads to the same love by dive travelers who use it.

I tried to include everything a dive traveler would need to plan a succesful trip to the Virgin Islands. However, prices, schedules and staff change, and I recommend calling operators and hotels before booking a flight. Please send any information (including updates, corrections, and new operators, hotels or dining establishments) that you feel should be added to the next edition to: Lynn Seldon Jr., c/o Hunter Publishing, 300 Raritan Center Parkway, Edison NJ 08818.

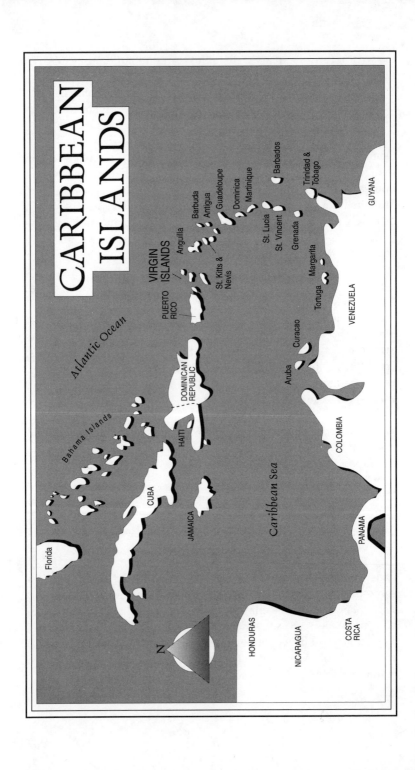

Contents

THE VIRGIN ISLANDS   1
  When To Go   2
  Weather   4
  Clothing   4
  Language   4
  Money   4
  Electricity   4
  Time   5
  Hours   5
  Travel Insurance   5
      DAN (Divers Alert Network)   8
      DSI (Diver's Security Information Network)   9
      ISDA (International Sport Divers Association)   10
      PADI (Professional Association of Diving Instructors) 11

BRITISH VIRGIN ISLANDS   15
  History   16
  Geography   17
  Tourism Offices   20
  Getting There   21
  Getting Around   22
  Mail   25
  Telephones   25
  Reading   25
  Health   25
  Diving   26
  Dive Operators   26
      Tortola   27
      Virgin Gorda   28
  Live-Aboards   28
  Photography   30
  Dive Sites   32
  Accommodations   36
      Tortola   37
      Virgin Gorda   41
      Anegada   43
      Cooper Island   44
      Guana Island   44
      Jost Van Dyke   45

Marina Cay   45
Mosquito Island   45
Peter Island   46
Dining   46
Tortola   46
Virgin Gorda   48
Anegada   49
Cooper Island   49
Jost Van Dyke   50
Marina Cay   50
Mosquito Island   50
Peter Island   50
Entertainment   50
Sightseeing   51
Tortola   51
Virgin Gorda   53
Anegada   54
Cooper Island   54
Jost Van Dyke   54
Marina Cay   56
Mosquito Island   56
Peter Island   56
Other Activities   56
Beaches   56
Boating   56
Fishing   57
Horseback Riding   57
Parasailing   57
Shopping   57
Snorkeling   58
Windsurfing   58

UNITED STATES VIRGIN ISLANDS   59
History   59
Geography   60
Tourism Offices   62
Getting There   63
Getting Around   65
Mail   67
Telephone   68
Reading   68
Health   68

Diving	68
Dive Operators	69
St. Croix	69
St. John	73
St. Thomas	75
Live-Aboards	78
Photography/Video	79
Dive Sites	80
St. Croix	82
St. John/St. Thomas	87
Accommodations	91
St. Croix	91
St. John	98
St. Thomas	103
Dining	109
St. Croix	109
Christiansted	109
Frederiksted	110
Elsewhere on St. Croix	110
St. John	111
Cruz Bay	111
Elsewhere on St. John	111
St. Thomas	112
Charlotte Amalie	112
Elsewhere on St. Thomas	112
Entertainment	113
Sightseeing	113
St. Croix	113
Christiansted	114
Frederiksted	115
Elsewhere on St. Croix	116
St. John	118
St. Thomas	121
Charlotte Amalie	125
Elsewhere on St. Thomas	127
Other Activities	128
Beaches	128
Boating	128
Fishing	129
Golf	129
Horseback Riding	130
Parasailing	130

Shopping	130
Snorkeling	131
Tennis	131
Windsurfing	131

Maps

Caribbean Islands	vi
The Virgin Islands	3
The British Virgin Islands	18
Dive Sites of the British Virgin Islands	31
Tortola	51
Virgin Gorda	55
The United States Virgin Islands	61
Dive Sites of St. Croix	81
Dive Sites of St. John & St. Thomas	88
St. Croix	117
St. John	119
St. Thomas	122
Charlotte Amalie	124

$\mathcal{T}$he $\mathcal{V}$irgin $\mathcal{I}$slands

$\mathcal{D}$ive travel in the Virgin Islands is different. Though not as popular here as on many other Caribbean islands, the dive travel difference lies in the diversity underwater and the vacation experience on land. The British and the United States Virgin Islands both offer history, beautiful scenery, fine dining, a wide variety of accommodations, entertainment and great diving, but the entire vacation experience is decidedly different in these two island groups.

Thanks to the British background and the ever-present sailing set, the BVI are tranquil and less harried than their US neighbors. If you want to get away from it all, above and below the surface, head for the BVI. This low-key lifestyle, however, comes at a higher price than a diving trip to St. John, St. Thomas, or St. Croix.

The USVI have grown into one of the world's top island destinations and, consequently, the locals here know how to cater to visitors. St. Thomas and, to a lesser degree, St. Croix have everything a traveler might want. St. John, however, is a BVI-style island in the USVI, with a more relaxed way of life. Competition has kept costs in the USVI fairly low.

You don't have to choose just one island or one group of islands. They are generally so close that you can "island-hop" from one to another as you mix and match to suit your tastes. The Virgin Islands have some of the highest return guest rates in the Caribbean and, once you discover a dive company or guest house you feel comfortable with, you'll go back time after time.

When planning a dive vacation, it's best to do business with a trusted travel agent or dive operator. If you have not used one before, take time to seek out someone you feel happy with. The best place to start is your local dive shop. They can often provide far more than flippers and many will be more than happy to help you plan a dive trip. Though each shop is different, you will find a common passion for underwater exploration. Make use of their expertise, contacts and competitive prices.

"Dive shops are a great resource for divers who want to travel," says Ralph Pearce, dive travel booking agent extraordinaire at Pan Aqua Diving in New York City. According to PADI International and the PADI Travel Network, Pan Aqua Diving books more trips than any other dive store in the world. "Dive shops can offer first-hand diving expertise, better service, low-price package deals, the best dive destinations, the right resorts, and dive operators they are familiar with," says Mr Pearce. In addition to regular equipment sales, Pan Aqua Diving averages three popular trips each month, providing packages that often include airfare, lodging, and diving. Dive shop personnel may even participate in the trip, offering training and certification.

You'll definitely receive invaluable advice at a dive shop, and you're likely to get a pretty good deal through them, too. Many stores and dive travel wholesalers make block bookings, which means a better price. This bulk discount is handed down to you, the customer. Try a few regular travel agents and compare the prices, but the chances are that you'll end up booking through a specialty dive store.

When To Go

Anytime is a great time for a dive trip to the Virgin Islands. The high season (meaning, generally, high prices) typically runs from mid-December to late-April. Other months are less crowded and certainly just as pretty. There is little change in water and air temperatures, although late summer and fall bring a higher chance of hurricanes and storms.

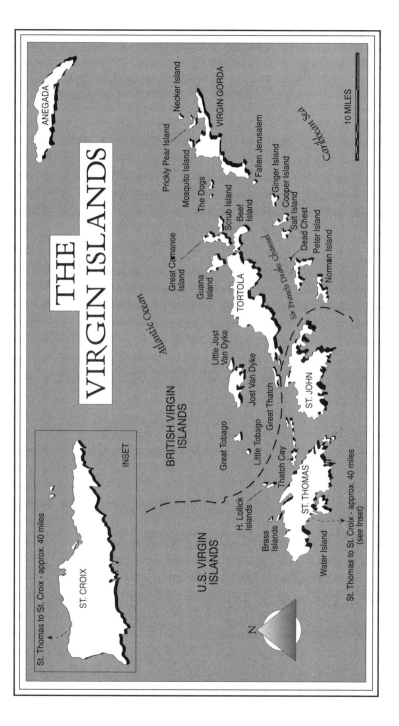

THE VIRGIN ISLANDS

ANEGADA

Necker Island

Prickly Pear Island

Mosquito Island

The Dogs

VIRGIN GORDA

Fallen Jerusalem

Ginger Island

Cooper Island

Scrub Island

Beef Island

Salt Island

Dead Chest

Peter Island

Norman Island

Great Camanoe Island

Guana Island

TORTOLA

Sir Francis Drake Channel

Atlantic Ocean

Little Jost Van Dyke

Jost Van Dyke

Great Thatch

ST. JOHN

Caribbean Sea

10 MILES

BRITISH VIRGIN ISLANDS

Great Tobago

Little Tobago

Thatch Cay

H. Lollick Islands

ST. THOMAS

Brass Islands

Water Island

U.S. VIRGIN ISLANDS

St. Thomas to St. Croix - approx. 40 miles (see Inset)

St. Thomas to St. Croix - approx. 40 miles

ST. CROIX

INSET

Weather

The islands enjoy wonderful weather year-round and average temperatures vary less than 5°F from winter to summer. The mean temperature in winter is 77°F; 82°F in summer, with cool trade winds. Summer also brings smaller crowds and good rates.

Water temperatures average a comfortable 80°F, but cooler winter waters may require some thermal protection for comfort.

Clothing

As with most things in the Caribbean, clothing is casual. In certain places, you may want to pack a jacket (no tie) for dining in some of the more exclusive restaurants (such as Little Dix Bay or Caneel Bay). A lightweight cotton sweater will also be useful for the cool evenings. Other than that, you can wear what you want. Bear in mind, however, that Virgin Islanders tend to dress conservatively when they're not on the beach.

Language

English is the official language. It is spoken with a beautiful West Indian and, in the BVI, British lilt. Once you get used to it, the language is easy to understand and a joy to hear.

Money

The official currency is the U.S. dollar. Travelers checks may be exchanged at banks and most hotels, while credit cards are generally accepted in hotels, restaurants, and shops. Personal checks are rarely accepted.

Electricity

The Virgin Islands use standard North American electrical service (120 volt/60 cycle).

Time

The Virgin Islands are in the Atlantic Standard Time Zone, which is one hour earlier than Eastern Standard Time.

Hours

Open hours for commercial operations are 9am to 5pm, Monday through Saturday. However, this can vary greatly. Many stores stay open later every night, while some stay open later only on Fridays. Some stores close earlier on Saturday, while others open their doors on Sundays when an infrequent cruise ship is in port.

Travel Insurance

Healthy divers travelers are happy divers. Underwater exploration can mean travel to some of the most interesting places in the world. However, it can also mean accidents and disease. Preparation is the key to any enjoyable dive vacation. From asking your local dive shop for help to remembering sea sickness medicine, preparation allows you to go in the know.

A safe dive trip starts with good travel plans. A good doctor, travel agent, dive shop, tour operator, or resort can save you time, money, and headaches. Divers should also consider refresher courses or dives prior to any major trip.

Once you find a good doctor, immunizations should be carefully considered and planned. They can only work if they are given at the right time and are not allowed to lapse. Travelers should check which immunizations are required and recommended for their destination(s).

The World Health Organization recommends that a five-year booster schedule be followed for routine immunizations, rather than the 10-year schedule followed in the U.S. This includes tetanus, diptheria, measles, mumps, rubella, and polio.

Many destinations have lowered immunization requirements and tourism offices tend to downplay potential diseases for travelers. However, it is important for dive travelers to learn about all possibilities and obtain proper vaccinations. Everyone should be immunized against tetanus. Other immunizations to consider include the new hepatitis A, the hepatitis B vaccine, typhoid vaccines, and rabies immunization.

Despite taking all the recommended precautions, you still may get sick abroad and there may not always be medication immediately available. Dive travelers should pack a medical kit in their luggage. At the very least, it should include first aid materials, antimalarial medication, diarrheal medicine, cold preparations, sunscreen, insect repellent, condoms, water purification tablets, a spare pair of prescription eyeglasses, sea sickness medicine, and a complete supply of any prescription or unusual medicines you may require.

Once safely at your dreamed-of dive destination, make sure you stay safe. Dive travel is inherently more risky than many other forms of travel, so it's important to follow a few safe practices.

Because many great dive sites are located in sunny spots, the first problem you'll encounter is warm weather. To avoid heat stroke or heat exhaustion, stay well hydrated, lightly clothed, avoid heavy exertion, and don't forget your sunscreen.

Preventable accidents are by far the most common cause of death and injury for travelers. Many people on vacation tend to become less safety-conscious than they are at home and this escapist attitude can cause accidents.

Eating and drinking, while enjoyable, can cause health problems. Traveler's diarrhea is the most common health complaint of tourists and can happen anywhere in the world. The best defense is to develop safe eating and drinking habits in risky areas. When it comes to liquids, let the drinker beware. Untreated water is not safe, but bottled water and other drinks (sealed) and alcoholic beverages (in moderation) are, generally, okay.

If Montezuma does take his revenge, it's best to react as quickly as possible. If you have a watery stool, take your temperature. If you are feverish (100°F or 37.7°C) or have a bloody stool, take only the antibiotic. If you do not have a fever or bloody stool, take the antibiotic and the anti-diarrheal. This will usually have you back in action within 15 hours. If symptoms do not improve within 48 hours, you will need medical attention because of the possibility of parasitic infection.

At the dive shop, on the dive boat, and underwater, don't let your guard down just because the diving is great. Make sure you understand any special safety requirements or practices for the destination, specific dive sites, and the dive operator. The more you know about the diving, the safer it will be.

Health/Emergencies/Medical Insurance

While the best insurance is safe diving, all divers should closely consider their current coverage. Divers who have health insurance generally find that certain dive-related injuries are already covered. But that does not mean divers don't need additional coverage.

Insurance companies will usually cover chamber treatments and other dive injuries in the U.S., but statistics show that a majority of dive injuries occur outside the country. Thus, dive-specific insurance coverage can be beneficial to divers not already covered and to those traveling overseas.

Check with your insurance company to see what coverage you currently have and whether or not you can buy additional coverage. The best bet is to buy additional coverage specifically geared for diving.

There are currently four major organizations offering dive insurance policies: Divers Alert Network (DAN), Diver's Security Network (DSI), International Sport Diver's Association (ISDA), and the Professional Association of Diving Instructors (PADI). To get proper coverage and additional benefits, contact all four and compare what each one offers. Each has unique cost structures and accompanying benefits.

DAN (Divers Alert Network)

DAN is based in Durham, North Carolina at the Duke University Medical Center. It was established in 1980 as an international non-profit organization dedicated to diver safety and supported by its members. Their research, worldwide network of diving medical experts, and chamber operators help thousands of injured divers each year. "When you join DAN, you support safety for everyone, but also for yourself," says Chris Wachholz, their director of development.

Currently, DAN membership provides a 24-hour Diving Emergency Hotline; a Diving Medicine & Safety Info Line; a Safe Diver Kit (DAN's Underwater Diving Accident Manual and tank decals); *Alert Diver*, DAN's bimonthly magazine; a personalized membership identification card; drawings for free equipment and dive trips; and an opportunity to promote and support safe diving worldwide. Membership currently costs $25 for individuals or $35 for families.

Additional DAN benefits include Assist America and a diving insurance program. Assist America, a global emergency evacuation service, means that any DAN member traveling more than 100 miles from home (whether insured or not) can be evacuated to an appropriate medical facility if the need arises. DAN members are covered – including medical and legal referrals, hospital fees, and other expenses – even if the problem is not dive-related. Once an injured diver is at an appropriate medical facility, it's up to the diver to pay for treatment. That's where additional coverage can help (through your current carrier, DAN, or another company).

- DAN's diving insurance program costs $25 per person each year and covers up to $40,000 (per calendar year) of treatment expenses worldwide for any in-water diving or snorkeling accident. This includes hyperbaric chamber treatment; physician and other fees for diagnostic and laboratory services and physiotherapy; and hospital care, services, and supplies for treatment of any in-water diving or snorkeling accident. After any other insurance you may have has paid its total of the bill, DAN pays 95% of all remaining eligible expenses.

Any recreational scuba diver or snorkeler (including instructors and divemasters supervising recreational diving activities) who is a resident of the U.S. or Canada is eligible for DAN diver insurance. If you don't already belong to DAN, you should definitely join.

> **DAN**
> Box 3823, Duke University Medical Center
> Durham, NC 27710
> (919) 684-2948 or (800) 446-2671 or (612) 588-2731 in MN
> Emergencies: (919) 684-8111

Along with insurance coverage, DAN provides an incredible array of additional services.

DSI (Diver's Security Information Network)

Based in Boulder, Colorado, DSI was formed by a group of divers in 1987 and has insured tens of thousands of divers since then. Their policies are provided by Capital Investors Life Insurance Company, based in Tampa, Florida.

DSI's new accident insurance policy is now available for divers and snorkelers, but also pays for injuries sustained while participating in most other watersports and boating activities. Hal Segal, president of DSI, feels the new policy recognizes that most divers also participate in other water-related activities and that family members often need coverage as well. He says, "Now you can choose from five levels of coverage, so you can pick just the coverages that you need."

- Class A covers all decompression-related injuries up to $15,000 for $25 per year. Most group health insurance plans either have exclusions or low coverage.

- Class B covers all injuries not related to decompression (e.g., cuts, bites, broken bones, and ear problems) up to $15,000 for $10 per year. Coverage starts when you break the water's surface and ends when you leave the water. This is especially important to divers who don't have a comprehensive health plan.

- Class C covers air ambulance and emergency evacuation expenses up to $15,000 for $5 a year. This is not covered by most health insurers.

- Class D covers other recreational watersports and boating injuries, including the time you are suiting up, removing gear, or handling equipment. Injuries sustained while skiing, sailing, fishing or recreational boating are included, while injuries during jetskiing, boat racing, and parasailing are excluded.

- Class E provides $40,000 of life insurance for death due to any covered injury for $20 per year.

A 5% deductible applies to all classes except E. According to DSI, the best combination for divers is A, B, C, and D, while the best combination for non-divers is C and D. Class E can be purchased with any other coverage. The minimum premium is $25 per year, regardless of the combination of coverages selected. Contact **DSI** at the following address:

> **DSI**
> 4800 Riverbend Road
> Boulder, CO 80301
> (303) 443-3600 or (800) 288-4810

ISDA (International Sport Divers Association)

The ISDA was formed in 1991 to preserve and protect the marine environment, promote recreational sport diving, and provide valuable services to its members. The ISDA Foundation provides funding for research grants, conservation programs, projects, and scholarships involved in the protection and preservation of the marine environment.

ISDA membership includes *BottomTime* newsletter; DiveGuard dive insurance; DiveReport dive site evaluations; GearGuard dive equipment theft protection; special dive trips; worldwide car rental discounts; diver ID kit and membership card; a Scuba Tuba signaling device; a Divers Card Visa for qualified members; and special photo processing discounts.

DiveGuard dive insurance, provided by American International Group, covers all diving accidents, as well as injuries occurring during the boat trip to and from dive sites provided by commercial dive operators and tender boat or zodiac dive trips taken from live-aboards. ISDA membership currently costs $49 and includes this insurance.

- Highlights of DiveGuard include up to $70,000 in benefits per occurrence ($10,000 for accidental death, $20,000 for accidental dismemberment, $10,000 for catastrophe cash, $20,000 for emergency evacuation, $2,000 for repatriation of remains, and $20,000 for accident medical reimbursements); a $250 deductible per occurrence; worldwide coverage; coverage of all in-water diving accidents; coverage for certified divers and students enrolled in certification courses in all 50 states; no physical examination required; benefits paid regardless of fault or negligence; emergency air evacuation and ambulance; medical and hospital expenses; recompression related diving injuries (chamber costs).

"It's best to compare the policies for benefits and costs and then make a personal decision," says Richard Ewing.

> **ISDA**
> Box 449
> Southport, CT 06490
> (203) 254-1213 or (800) 766-4940

PADI (Professional Association of Diving Instructors)

For the first time, a certifying agency recently started offering dive accident insurance coverage for students and divers. PADI's Diver Accident Program offers insurance to students taking their PADI Open Water Diver course and coverage for upper-level training and non-training diving activities.

- The student coverage provides up to $25,000 in dive accident compensation related to medical treatment, emergency evacuation expenses, lost equipment, death, disability, and repatriation. This unique program also covers students as they are being transported to and from the open water training sites. The certified diver coverage is similar to the student coverage, but has a $40,000 limit. The policy is currently $29 annually, with no deductible.

• The PADI Diver Accident Program also benefits the Divers Alert Network (DAN) and Project AWARE (Aquatic World Awareness, Responsibility, and Education) Foundation. A portion of each program fee helps DAN operate its diver emergency service and helps fund environmental research grants available through the Project AWARE Foundation. Divers may also sign up for the PADI Diver Accident Program and join DAN at the same time, saving $5 off the program fee.

"DAN provides a very valuable service to the dive industry," says John Cronin, PADI's Chief Executive Officer. "As an industry leader in education and safety, it's appropriate for PADI to take the lead in supporting DAN's programs and studies." Contact Your Local **PADI Dive Center** or write:

> **PADI**
> 1251 E. Dyer Road #100
> Santa Ana, CA 92705-5605
> (714) 540-7234

The best insurance against injury is to be a safe diver. But accidents do happen and divers should make sure they have the right coverage.

Publications and Other Sources of Information

> **Centers for Disease Control and Prevention (CDC)**
> **Traveler's Information Hotline:** (404) 332-4559
>
> **Health Information for International Travel**
> **HHS Publication No. [CDC] 90-8280** ($5)
> Supt. of Documents, Government Printing Office
> Washington, DC 20402
> (202) 783-3238

**International Association for Medical Assistance
to Travellers (IAMAT)**
417 Center Street
Lewiston, NY 14092
(716) 754-4883

British Virgin Islands

*I*f you're looking for a quiet Caribbean destination, look no further than the British Virgin Islands. Yet to be discovered by the traveling masses, the BVI still live up to their name as virgin territory.

Long known as a sailor's paradise, the mainly volcanic, emerald-like islands are surrounded by sapphire-blue seas and offer incredible scenery above and below the water line. Gentle breezes keep temperatures at a steady 80-90°, making the diving and sailing comfortable year-round.

More than 60 islands make up the BVI, though only a handful are inhabited. Tortola is the largest and is home to the capital of Road Town. The island has more than 17,000 residents and boasts several marinas filled with the yachts that account for nearly half the tourist "beds" available in the BVI. Linked to Tortola by a toll bridge is Beef Island, which houses the International Airport. An efficient ferry service (including a short hop by light aircraft in some cases) takes visitors to the other main islands of Virgin Gorda, Jost Van Dyke, and magical Anegada. The other islands in this archipelago are Cooper Island, Ginger Island, The Dogs, Great Camanoe, Necker Island, Guana Island, Mosquito Island, and Eustatia Island.

There are no casinos or high-rise hotels and apartments in the BVI, just a few nightclubs and discos. Walking or hiking in the fresh air and watersports are the main activities, so early to bed and early to rise is more common than dancing the night away. This leaves plenty of time to discover some of "Nature's Little Secrets" above and below the surface.

The BVI have always remained in the background as a diving destination and, consequently, the underwater world has not been so exploited here as on other Caribbean islands. That is not to say that there is less to see here. To the contrary, the BVI offer a wide variety of diving experiences as well as incredible peace and quiet on land.

History

Since Columbus first spotted the British Virgin Islands in 1493, adventurers have been held spellbound by their unspoiled beauty. Likening them to the legendary St. Ursula surrounded by her 11,000 Virgins, Christopher Columbus supposedly anchored off Virgin Gorda (the fat virgin) and so named the whole group.

Many famous seafarers later passed through the islands, including Sir Francis Drake. The channel that cuts through the center of the islands now bears Drake's name. Dutch buccaneers settled the islands in the 17th century, followed by the English, and the group was later raided by the Spanish. It was not until the 18th century that the British gained a firm hold on the islands.

Local folklore maintains that infamous pirates rampaged the waters, largely unaffected by developments on land. Norman Island is reputed to be the setting for Robert Louis Stevenson's fictional *Treasure Island*, where the real pirate, Blackbeard, supposedly anchored off Deadman's Bay. After one particularly successful raid, while he and his men split the "booty," an argument arose and he marooned 15 men on the nearby island of Dead Chest with just a bottle of rum and their sea chests for company. Hence the mariner's song, *"Fifteen men on dead man's chest, Yo ho ho and a bottle of rum!"* Some locals believe there is still treasure to be found here, either buried on land or in the many wrecks that line the seabed.

In 1872, the islands were admitted as a separate colony under the Leeward Islands Administration and, by the turn of the century, were developing their own banks, hospitals, and schools. The island's residents are fiercely proud of their British heritage. One of the most politically stable territories in the Caribbean and still a colony of the United Kingdom, the BVI have their own elected Chief Minister, government, and a resident British Governor appointed by the Queen.

Tourism did not touch the islands until the mid-1960s, when Laurence Rockefeller developed Little Dix Bay on Virgin Gorda. This was followed by the opening of The Moorings in 1969, a company that heralded the start of the now-booming charter yacht business. Of course, dive operators were close behind.

The BVI remain remarkably undeveloped in comparison to neighboring Puerto Rico and the USVI, although plans are underway to increase tourism through carefully controlled development and improvements in transportation facilities. With industry and commerce on the islands now split almost equally between tourism and the flourishing offshore financial sector, BVI residents are keen to see their islands develop as a destination for discerning dive travelers.

Geography

The BVI's tourism slogan is "Nature's Little Secrets" and it's easy to see why. Pride runs deep in the fact that these unspoiled islands offer a wonderful opportunity to discover hidden natural splendors. Much of what the region has to offer is preserved for today's visitors and for future generations in 11 areas managed by the BVI National Parks Trust. The Trust's goal of establishing 12 or more sections in the next few decades is a dream every BVI islander shares with enthusiasm.

The National Parks of the British Virgin Islands began in the 1960s, when the Rockefellers made a gift of three sites to the BVI government: Sage Mountain on Tortola and Devil's Bay and Spring Bay on Virgin Gorda. Reforestation has been continuing in the 92-acre Sage Mountain National Park since that time. The reintroduction of vegetation that had disappeared from the island has returned the landscape to what Tortola may have looked like when Columbus first saw it in 1493.

THE BRITISH VIRGIN ISLANDS

N

ANEGADA

Atlantic Ocean

Caribbean Sea

Great Tobago
Little Tobago

Jost Van Dyke

Little Jost
Van Dyke

Great Thatch

Great Camanoe
Island

Guana
Island

TORTOLA

Scrub
Island

Beef Island

The Dogs

Mosquito Island

Prickly Pear Island

Necker Island

VIRGIN GORDA

Fallen Jerusalem

Ginger Island

Cooper Island

Salt Island

Dead Chest

Peter Island

Norman Island

Sir Francis Drake Channel

10 MILES

At 1,780 feet, Sage Mountain is the highest point in both the BVI and the USVI and views from its hiking trails are breathtaking. (Check the "Reading" section for an excellent resource guide to hiking in the Caribbean.) Just as rewarding is the vegetation of huge broadleafed elephant ear philodendrons and lacy ferns growing in the shade of mahogany, manilkara, and white cedar trees. Color is added to the scene by exquisite red flowers and yellow stalks of palicourea and the rose-like blossoms of coco-plum. Hummingbirds flit among the trees and mockingbirds remind visitors that they are not alone, although solitude is one of the pleasures of Sage Mountain (and the rest of the BVI).

Rhone National Marine Park is centered around the Wreck of the *RMS Rhone* (see "Dive Sites"), creating one of the best and most well-preserved dive sites in the Caribbean. When divers come to the surface, they can explore Dead Chest Island, which is also part of the park. The island's cliffs, covered by cactus, sage, and frangipani, are favorite nesting sites for terns, nod-dies, and other sea birds. Its salt ponds are rimmed by the black mangrove. Colorful Blonde Rock (see "Dive Sites") is also within Rhone National Maritime Park.

J.R. O'Neal Botanic Gardens in the center of Road Town on Tortola highlight the brilliant color to be found on dry land here. The gardens, which cover three-acres, were created by the BVI National Parks Trust and developed by an enthusiastic group of local volunteers. Plants are arranged according to habitat, in sections accessed by landscaped paths radiating from a three-tiered fountain. The orchid house and a small rainforest are reached by crossing a charming lily pond. Other paths lead to a cactus garden and a palm grove. The gardens are filled with such flowering plants and shrubs as hibiscus, bougainvillea, and the vibrant scarlet flowers of the aptly-named flamboyant tree.

The one secret Mother Nature is keeping to herself is the origin of the giant boulders that make The Baths and Devil's Bay National Park one of the BVI's most popular destinations. The huge rocks that are strewn along the beach on Virgin Gorda's southwest shore are granite, a stone not usually found south of the Carolinas. Whether they were placed there by some race of giants, moved south by an ancient glacier, or spewed up by the volcanoes that created the islands eons ago is an unsolved mystery. Regardless of the rocks' origin, the cave-like passages and hidden pools between them invite adventure.

Except for the one special island of Anegada, the volcanic action that created the BVI has left rocks, boulders and dramatic cliff-sides on its more than 60 islands. Anegada, the most northerly island of the archipelago, is a flat 15 square miles of coral and sand surrounded by reefs. The animal population here includes some 2,000 wild goats, donkeys, and cattle, and a small population of endangered rock iguana. The reptile, which looks fierce but is quite harmless, grows to a length of five feet and can weigh up to 20 pounds. The BVI National Parks Trust is planning to create a sanctuary for the Anegada iguanas and has already established a colony of flamingos in a 1,100-acre bird sanctuary on one of Anegada's salt ponds. The sanctuary is also a protected nesting ground for several varieties of heron, as well as ospreys and a species of tern that has been spending the summer in the BVI for centuries.

From the depths of the Caribbean to the shores of Anegada, the BVI are waiting to be discovered by dive travelers.

Tourism Offices

For basic information and informative brochures, call (800) 835-8530 (New York) or (800) 232-7770. For more detailed information and advice, contact the office of the British Virgin Islands Tourist Board nearest you:

370 Lexington Ave.
New York, NY 10017
(212) 696-0400

1686 Union St., Ste. 305
San Francisco, CA 94123
(415) 775-0344

PO Box 134
Road Town
Tortola, BVI
(809) 494-3134

Getting There

By Air

The BVI aren't among the easiest islands in the Caribbean to reach, but that has kept tourism development and encroachment to a minimum. Many of the airlines (and other tour operators) offer a variety of money-saving packages, which include airfare, accommodations, and much more. Airlines change their service often, so it's best to check all options.

Connections are generally made through San Juan, Puerto Rico or St. Thomas, USVI. These stopovers give you the opportunity to extend your vacation and explore these U.S. islands easily.

Service to San Juan and St. Thomas is provided by **American Airlines**, (800) 433-7300; **Continental Airlines**, (800) 231-0856; **Delta Airlines**, (800) 221-1212; and **USAir**, (800) 428-4322.

From San Juan, **American Eagle**, (800) 327-8376, flies to Tortola and **Sunaire Express**, 495-2480 or (800) 524-2094, flies to Tortola and Virgin Gorda. From St. Thomas, **Sunaire Express**, 495-2480 or (800) 524-2094, flies to Tortola. **LIAT**, 462-0701, and **Gorda Aero Service**, 495-2271, also provide service to and from other Caribbean islands.

By Sea

Because the BVI offer some of the finest sailing waters in the world, they are easy to reach by boat. Ships of all sizes call and sail in the BVI, including a number of ferries that connect St. Thomas with the BVI. **Native Son**, 495-4617, and **Smiths Ferry Services**, 494-4430, offer service between St. Thomas, Tortola, and Virgin Gorda. In addition, **Inter-Island Boat Services**, 776-6597, runs ferries between St. John and Tortola.

Entry/Departure Regulations

It's usually easy to enter and leave the BVI. Though it's not required, a U.S. passport is always the best form of identification for U.S. citizens. Other forms of identification are accepted, such as a driver's license, voter's card, or birth certificate. If you plan to travel outside the BVI, you must have a birth certificate or passport. Citizens of other countries should follow whatever the BVI require for their country. There are no special health restrictions for those entering from the mainland U.S. or Puerto Rico.

Though not nearly the shopping hotspot that the USVI have become, the BVI still provide a wide array of interesting (and relatively inexpensive) shopping possibilities.

Duty-free Allowances

U.S. residents are allowed a duty-free shopping quota of $600. A flat rate of 10% is charged on any purchases over this limit, up to a maximum of $1,000 more. U.S. citizens can also take back up to 200 cigarettes, 100 (non-Cuban) cigars, and those 21 years or older can take one liter of liquor. U.S. residents can also mail an unlimited number of gifts to friends (other than perfume, liquor, and tobacco), each worth $50 or less.

Getting Around

By Air

There's really not much reason to travel by air between islands in the BVI. Everything is close and easily reached by boat. However, **Sunaire Express**, 495-2480, offers service between Tortola and Virgin Gorda. **Gorda Aero Service**, 495-2271, offers flights between Tortola and Anegada, as well a charter service.

By Sea

Travel between (and even on) islands is often easiest by boat. Frequent regular service and a number of unscheduled boat rides are available. Between Tortola and Virgin Gorda, contact **North Sound Express**, 494-2746, or **Speedy's Fantasy**, 495-5240. To get to Jost Van Dyke, contact **Jost Van Dyke Ferry Service** at 494-2997. Many resorts on the other remote islands provide boat transportation for arriving passengers or arrange for ferry service.

By Car

Boats are a great way to get around, but rental cars are highly recommended as they often lead to more interesting excursions, even if just for a day or two. They also offer the most flexible means of transportation. Just remember that, as a remnant of British rule, traffic keeps to the left. You'll need a valid driver's license to rent a car.

Recommended car rental agencies on Tortola include: **Budget**, 494-2639; **Hertz**, 495-4405; and **National**, 494-3197. On Virgin Gorda, several taxi companies also rent jeeps (ideal for the island): **Andy's Taxi Service and Jeep Rental**, 495-5252; **Mahogany Rentals and Taxi Service**, 495-5469; and **Speedy's Taxi Service**, 495-5234.

By Bus

For a great BVI experience, take the bus on Tortola. You'll meet locals and see the island at their pace. Contact **Scato's Bus Service** at 494-2364.

By Taxi

Friendly taxi drivers offer a great way to get around the islands if you're not on a tight budget. Fares are government-regulated and are based on the destination, rather than the number of passengers (drivers often try to get additional passengers for airport pickups). Expect to pay about $15 for a shorter trip and $30 for a longer one.

On Tortola, contact the **BVI Taxi Association** at 495-2378. On Virgin Gorda, contact **Mahogany Taxi Service** at 495-5469. On other islands, it's best by boat.

Calendar of Events/Holidays

JANUARY   New Year's Day (public holiday)
              BVI Agricultural Week, 495-2532

FEBRUARY   Botanical Gardens Art Show, 494-4557

MARCH   Charity Fishing Tournament, 494-3286
              Botanical Gardens Horticultural Society Show,
                 494-4557
              Virgin Gorda Festival, (800) 835-8530
              Commonwealth Day (public holiday)

APRIL   Good Friday (public holiday)
              Spring Regatta, 494-3286

MAY   Spring Caribbean Arts Festival, 495-4252

JUNE   White Monday (public holiday)
              Sovereign's Birthday (public holiday)

JULY   Territory Day (public holiday)

AUGUST   BVI Summer Festival, 494-2875

SEPTEMBER   International Rugby Festival, (800) 835-8530
              Wooden Boat Regatta, (800) 835-8530

OCTOBER   Bacardi Rum Beach Party, 495-4639

NOVEMBER   BVI Boat Show, 494-3286
              Fast Tacks, 494-2746
              Birthday of the Heir to the Throne
                 (public holiday)

DECEMBER   Christmas Day (public holiday)

Mail

There are post offices only in Road Town and Spanish Town and mail service to and from the U.S. is not quick. If you're in a hurry, contact **Rush It In Road Town** at 494-4421 or **Rush It In Spanish Town** at 495-5821.

Telephones

There is excellent service between the BVI (area code 809) and the rest of the world. While in the islands, you only need to dial the last five numerals of a local phone number.

Reading

Any vacation experience can be enhanced by further background reading before and during a trip. For a humorous look at Caribbean life, there's nothing better than Herman Wouk's *Don't Stop the Carnival*. For BVI background, find a copy of *Concise History of the British Virgin Islands*, by Vernon Pickering. Harry Pariser's *Adventure Guide to the Virgin Islands* gives excellent overall coverage, including history and politics. Avid hikers should pick up a copy of *The Caribbean: A Walking & Hiking Guide*, by Leonard M. Adkins. The local newspaper in the BVI is the *Island Sun*.

Health

For health emergencies, call 999 or contact individual hospitals on the two major islands. On Tortola, call the **hospital** at 494-3497. On Virgin Gorda, call the **Spanish Town Clinic** at 495-5337 or the **North Sound Clinic** at 495-7310. See the "Travel Insurance" section in the Introduction for companies specializing in dive travel insurance.

Diving

Diving in the BVI is special. Though not as well known as other Caribbean or worldwide diving destinations, the diving can be as good and as interesting as anywhere in the world. Diverse diving and many topside attractions make the BVI one of the best spots for smart dive travelers.

Diving conditions are typically ideal for all experience levels, with warm water, calm seas, and excellent visibility. Many of the reefs and wrecks of the BVI are in relatively shallow water.

All operators will require presentation of your C-card, while some may request a review of your logbook or check-out dive. As with most destinations, a PADI C-card is the most-recognized certification of your abilities, but many other forms are accepted. The BVI also offer a great place to complete your certification process, including entire courses or check-out dives.

The nearest recompression chamber is on St. Thomas in the USVI.

Dive Operators

Like the USVI, BVI dive operators love exposing dive travelers to the diving off their islands. They are all friendly and generally more relaxed and less busy than many operators on more dive-intensive islands in the Caribbean.

With so many excellent operators, it's easy to choose one or more companies for their convenience, offerings, and style. A wide array of packages that include diving, accommodations, dining, and more can make per-dive costs much lower. You may want to try dives with a few operators and then purchase a package with your favorite one.

Tortola

Baskin in the Sun
Prospect Reef Resort, Roadtown
Tortola, British Virgin Islands
494-3858 or (800) 233-7938
FAX 494-5653

Baskin in the Sun
Soper's Hole West End
Tortola, British Virgin Islands
495-4582 or (800) 233-7938
FAX 494-5853

Baskin in the Sun
Village Cay Inner Harbor, Road Town
Tortola, British Virgin Islands
494-4956 or (800) 233-7938
FAX 494-4304

Comments: Masterfully run by Alan Jardine, Baskin in the Sun is one of the top operators in the BVI. With more than 20 years of BVI excellence, repeat divers are the norm and it's easy to see why, with three Tortola locations, people choose this excellent company. They have enough boats, locations, and dives to provide a good range of diving experiences to anyone staying on Tortola or outlying islands. They offer a wide variety of hotel/dive packages, great service, and superior diving.

Blue Water Divers
PO Box 846, Road Town
Tortola, British Virgin Islands
494-2847 or (800) 233-7938
FAX 494-0198

Comments: This personalized operation is run by Keith and Mike Royle. It is conveniently located at Nanny Cay Marina and divers love the small, intimate dive trips. They offer a selection of hotel and diving packages, with flexible schedules and dive sites.

Underwater Safaris
Wickham's Cay II, Road Town
Tortola, British Virgin Islands
494-3235 or (800) 537-7032
FAX 494-5322

Comments: Conveniently located at The Moorings – Mariner Inn and at Cooper Island Beach Club – this large operator runs a number of boats and offers packages with or without accommodations.

Virgin Gorda

Dive B.V.I.
Virgin Gorda Yacht Harbour
Virgin Gorda, British Virgin Islands
495-5513 or (800) 848-7078
FAX 495-5347

Comments: This large and friendly company is a Virgin Gorda diving favorite. With three locations and a selection of packages with or without hotel accommodations included, BVI dive travelers can't go wrong.

Kilbride's Underwater Tours
Bitter End Yacht Club & Resort
PO Box 46, North Sound
Virgin Gorda, BVI
495-9638 or (800) 932-4286
FAX 495-7549

Comments: Founded long ago by Caribbean diving pioneer Bert Kilbride, this legendary BVI dive operation is now owned and run by his Floridian partner, Mike Van Blaricum. It's still a perfect diving choice, serving Bitter End and many other Virgin Gorda hotel guests. Mike has perfected the service and diving at Kilbride's Underwater Tours, making it an ideal diving base.

Live-Aboards

The closeness of the BVI, as well as St. John and St. Thomas, make the Virgin Islands ideal for live-aboard dive vacations.

Though many boats and operators offer diving, living aboard a boat to dive is a unique experience.

Club Med 1
7975 N. Hayden Rd.
Scottsdale, AZ 85258
(800) 258-2633

Comments: This 191-cabin sailing cruise ship is a wonderful way to tour the Caribbean, with as much diving as you want thrown in for good measure. Three days out of this wonderful seven-day cruise are spent in the waters of the Virgin Islands (both BVI and USVI). The ship sails out of Martinique and offers a unique scuba diving adventure, with lots of extras.

Cuan Law
Box 4065, Road Town
Tortola, BVI
648-3393 or (800) 648-3393
FAX 494-5774

Comments: This 105-foot trimaran is targeted at scuba divers, but a wide variety of watersports and other activities is available. It's based in Road Town, Tortola, but heads throughout the BVI for some spectacular diving at the sites mentioned below and many more. Ten spacious cabins and all possible boating and diving amenities make this a special BVI dive travel option.

The owners, Duncan and Annie Muirhead, have made the *Cuan Law* one of the best live-aboard possibilities in the entire Caribbean. The friendly staff, great food, fun atmosphere, and the flexible diving ensure a great experience for first-time or repeat BVI divers.

Irie Dive & Sail Charters
5100 Long Bay Road, Flagship
St. Thomas, USVI 00802
774-5630
FAX 776-3074

Divers looking for a great way to explore the Virgin Islands will love *Irie*. Based in St. Thomas, this 46-foot sailing vessel provides a unique diving and sailing vacation in the crystal-clear waters of the USVI and the BVI.

Irie's crew are both dive instructors and know the best dive sites on every island. The sailing and diving make for a great combination.

> **Regency Yacht Vacations**
> 5200 Long Bay Road
> St. Thomas, USVI 00802
> 776-5950 or (800) 524-7676
> FAX 776-7631

Comments: Based in St. Thomas, Regency Yacht Vacations represents hundreds of yachts in the Virgin Islands, many of which offer dive charters. Charter consultant Michon Willman is experienced at working with divers and can help them choose the right boat. The choices include *Irie* (see above), *Whisper* (a 44' sailing ship owned and captained by Gwen Hamlin), and many others. Diving takes place throughout the Virgin Islands.

Photography

Most operators still photography and video options. It's best to call ahead to check on programs, instruction, rentals, and development. If you're serious about underwater photography and video, be sure to contact:

> **Rainbow Visions**
> Box 680, Road Town
> Tortola, BVI
> 494-2749

Comments: The Rainbow Visions Photo Center and Gallery was started in 1986 by Jim and Idile Scheiner. Their store and gallery is adjacent to the Baskin in the Sun at Prospect Reef Resort. They also have a studio and office next to Treasure Isle Resort. In addition to serving the clients of Baskin in the Sun, they provide photography and video services for Underwater Safaris, Blue Water Divers, Dive BVI, and *Cuan Law*. Their work has been widely purchased and published.

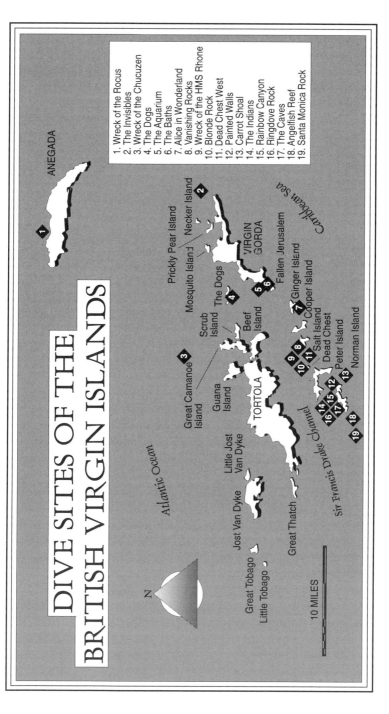

DIVE SITES OF THE BRITISH VIRGIN ISLANDS

1. Wreck of the Rocus
2. The Invisibles
3. Wreck of the Chucuzen
4. The Dogs
5. The Aquarium
6. The Baths
7. Alice in Wonderland
8. Vanishing Rocks
9. Wreck of the HMS Rhone
10. Blonde Rock
11. Dead Chest West
12. Painted Walls
13. Carrot Shoal
14. The Indians
15. Rainbow Canyon
16. Ringdove Rock
17. The Caves
18. Angelfish Reef
19. Santa Monica Rock

ANEGADA

Atlantic Ocean

Caribbean Sea

Great Tobago
Little Tobago

Jost Van Dyke

Little Jost
Van Dyke

Great Thatch

Great Camanoe
Island

Guana
Island

TORTOLA

Scrub
Island

Beef
Island

Mosquito Island

The Dogs

Prickly Pear Island Necker Island

VIRGIN
GORDA

Fallen Jerusalem

Ginger Island

Cooper Island

Salt Island

Dead Chest

Peter Island

Norman Island

Sir Francis Drake Channel

N

10 MILES

Dive Sites

The BVI lie at the edge of a huge underwater shelf that extends some 85 miles from Puerto Rico before dropping off in the Atlantic to the north and the Caribbean to the south. Most of the sport diving in the BVI is on that shelf, where many fascinating wrecks and spectacular underwater formations are at a reasonable depth for divers.

The compactness of the BVI is a big advantage. The entire chain extends for 35 miles along Sir Francis Drake Channel and even dive sites considered remote are within a half-hour of the islands of Tortola or Virgin Gorda. The sheltering effect of the islands cuts the wind speed at most sites. Summer and winter temperatures in the BVI are relatively the same above and below the surface.

The following review of potential dive sites in the BVI should serve only as a guide to which dives might interest certain divers. Keep in mind that conditions change. The descriptions, depths, and levels of expertise needed are given only as guidelines. A local dive operator should always be consulted for up-to-date information about dive sites and current conditions.

Preparation is the key to safe and enjoyable diving. Be sure your equipment has been properly serviced and set up. If you haven't been diving recently, you may want to consider a refresher course or dive, as well as any additional training while you're in the BVI.

Conservation is the key to the future enjoyment of diving in the BVI and elsewhere. Divers should adhere to all accepted and local rules and etiquette for preserving the reef. Take only pictures and leave only bubbles.

1. Wreck of the *Rocus*, Anegada (20'-40'; novice to expert): Unlike the rest of the tropical and mountainous BVI, Anegada is a flat and rather barren island. The great diving is just being explored and the wreck of the *Rocus* provides a perfect introduction to the wide variety of wrecks and reef formations off Anegada's coast. This freighter sank in 1929 and has thus broken apart in some places. However, it has also had time to mature, with lots of colorful coral and a wide variety of passing fish. Unless you're staying on the Anegada, this is a special trip for most BVI dive operators.

2. The Invisibles, Virgin Gorda (10'-60'; intermediate to expert): These stunning pinnacles off Virgin Gorda offer one of the best dives in the BVI. Though the boat ride out can be rough, it's well worth it whenever a dive operator makes a trip to The Invisibles. The pinnacles rise from the bottom to within a few feet of the surface and attract an incredible variety and quantity of fish. Every dive here is different, thanks to the many encounters with passing fish.

3. Wreck of the *Chikuzen*, Virgin Gorda (35'-75'; intermediate to expert): This large ship, lying about nine miles off the coast of Virgin Gorda, is a special wreck dive. The *Chikuzen* was sunk intentionally in 1981 and is now packed with coral life. The full 246-foot length of this vessel is teeming with fish of every description. Divers may see big rays, horse-eye jacks, barracudas, and much more. Its sheer size in open sea also serves to attract a large number of fish. From seemingly thousands of barracuda to many other schools of fish, the *Chikuzen* is well worth the boat ride.

4. The Dogs, between Tortola and Virgin Gorda (20'-60'; novice to expert): These rocky islands are a popular and convenient destination for many BVI operators. There are several excellent dive sites, including Joe's Cave and The Chimneys (named after a colorful soft coral reef formation located at the end of a pretty tunnel). The southern side of Great Dog is a good spot for beginners, where divers swim along the parallel reef.

5. The Aquarium, Virgin Gorda (15'-35'; novice to expert): As you can guess, this convenient and easy dive is usually packed with fish. Located just off Virgin Gorda's Spanish Town, it's a great first dive.

6. The Baths, Virgin Gorda (0'-35'; novice to expert): Though these stunning rock formations are better known as a great snorkeling and land exploration site, the diving here can be quite interesting. Boat traffic can get quite heavy, so special attention is required. The area around Devil's Bay can be exciting and The Baths is simply one of the best snorkeling sites in the Caribbean.

7. Alice in Wonderland, Ginger Island (15'-100'; intermediate to expert): This pretty dive off Ginger Island can be beautiful on a calm day. The site is known for its giant star corals and other colorful coral scenery. Huge mushroom-shaped corals give the site its name.

8. Vanishing Rocks, Salt Island (20'-50'; intermediate to expert): Just off Salt Island, this site is also called Dry Rocks West (though they're not always dry). The heavy current can make it a difficult or impossible dive, but that same current provides lots of coral and fish life all around the rocks.

9. Wreck of the *RMS Rhone*, Salt Island (15'-80'; intermediate to expert): Every diver in the Virgin Islands should visit the wreck of the *Rhone* at least once. Once you dive it, you'll want to return often.

Made famous by the feature film, *The Deep,* this dive is even better than its reputation. The 310-foot steel-hulled ship sunk in a storm and split it two, with only a few survivors.

RMS Rhone has had plenty of time to develop into a mature artificial reef, with lots of colorful coral and fish. Because it's in two distinct parts, it's a popular two-tank dive for both BVI and USVI operators.

The deeper bow section provides lots of places to explore inside and outside the ship. Divers will enjoy the coral-encrusted cargo hold and other interior chambers. Outside, a careful survey of the wreckage reveals the ship's foremast, complete with crow's nest, and its bowsprit lying in the sand. The shallower stern section includes a giant ship's propeller, the once-powerful engine, her prop shaft, and several boilers.

The *Rhone* plays host to dozens of divers and snorkelers daily. It has been a National Park since 1980 and deserves its status as one of the premier dives in the world.

10. Blonde Rock, Dead Chest Island* (5'-60'; intermediate to expert): This pinnacle dive draws its name from the yellow fire coral at its peak. The large rock features many caves and undercuts, with lots of hiding places for a wide variety of marine life, including moray eels, crabs, beautiful fan corals, hordes of reef fish, and lobster.

11. Dead Chest West, Dead Chest Island (20'-60'; novice to expert): This interesting and easy dive is located between Dead Chest Island and Peter Island. There is a good selection of formations and fish.

12. Painted Walls, Norman Island (20'-50'; intermediate to expert): The vertical portions of this dive are a colorful cornucopia and that's how the site got its name. Divers will delight at the kaleidoscope of colors created by encrusting corals and sponges on the walls of four long gullies. With typically excellent visibility, this is a diver and operator favorite in the BVI.

13. Carrot Shoal, Norman Island (10'-60'; intermediate to expert): This large ridge dive is filled with hiding places. There are generally lots of colorful fish swimming around.

14. The Indians, Norman Island (10'-50'; novice to expert): These pinnacles off Norman Island are easy to find and offer many excellent dives (as well as good snorkeling). The four tooth-like formations yield a series of canyons and grottoes, which feature both soft and hard corals. The rocks also serve as beacons for many passing fish. The pinnacles usually offer an easy dive and a fun round-the-rock exploration.

15. Rainbow Canyon, Norman Island (15'-50'; novice to expert): This popular and colorful dive is ideal for all levels. Large coral heads are interspersed throughout the site, creating busy areas for marine life (and exploring divers). This is a colorful and easy introductory BVI dive.

16. Ringdove Rock, Norman Island (10'-60'; novice to expert): Another easy introductory BVI dive, Ringdove Rock is a great pinnacle to explore. The rock face features lots of nooks and crannies for eels and lobster, as well as stunning coral formations. Busy Ringdove Rock is also a draw to many passing fish.

17. The Caves, Norman Island (0'-60'; beginner to expert): Though this Norman Island site is known for its great snorkeling, it also offers an unusual dive. There are three shallow caves divers and snorkelers can explore, featuring lots of coral that can (and should) be illuminated by lights. The reef sloping offshore is an added bonus.

18. Angelfish Reef, Norman Island (20'-90'; intermediate): Divers will soon discover that this pretty reef off Norman Island is a heavenly mix of angelfish and other colorful marine life. The reef features several ridges and floors with a lively array of coral formations.

19. Santa Monica Rock, Norman Island (10'-100'; intermediate to expert): Yet another pretty pinnacle dive site, Santa Monica Rock is one of the larger pinnacle dives in the BVI and deserves several visits for dedicated divers. As with similar sites in the area, Santa Monica Rock features lots of coral and passing fish. Because it is on the outer edge of the island chain, this is a great place to see larger open ocean (pelagic) fish, like spotted eagle rays and nurse sharks. The visibility and amount of exploration and viewing opportunities make this a BVI favorite.

Accommodations

One of the beauties about vacationing in the BVI is the variety of experiences above and below the surface. This especially applies to accommodations options. Though certain resorts do cater to divers and many of these are highlighted below, it's easy to stay at a hotel that doesn't specialize, while still enjoying the great diving.

It's difficult to categorize pricing for BVI accommodations and it becomes an even greater task when diving and diving packages are involved. The following accommodation options provide a general cost idea. They are rated as follows:

> Inexpensive: less than $100
> Moderate: $100 to $200
> Expensive: more than $200

These prices relate to an average in-season standard double room for two and do not include any diving, dining, or other package options. Remember that prices can drop dramatically with package deals and during the off-season (May to November). Use the rates listed here as a very general guideline. It's best to check with several places to get the best possible price and experience. Always call ahead to check current rates and to see if any special deals are being offered.

Tortola

Brewers Bay Campground
Box 185, Road Town
Tortola, BVI
776-6226

Comments: This is one of few pure budget choices in the BVI. Bare and prepared sites are available for a minimal charge. Basic campground amenities and friendly people make this a perfect cheap choice. Inexpensive.

Hotel Castle Maria
PO Box 206, Road Town
Tortola, BVI
494-2553 or 494-4255

Comments: Ideally situated right in Road Town, this is a nice lower-budget choice. There is a selection of accommodations options, as well as simple amenities and good service. Inexpensive.

Fort Recovery Villas
West End
Tortola, BVI
495-4467

Comments: This well-run enclave of one- , two- , three- , and four-bedroom villas overlooks the Sir Francis Drake Channel. These perfect getaway villas all have great views, living rooms, and kitchens. Moderate to Expensive.

Frenchman's Cay Resort Hotel
PO Box 1054, West End
Tortola, BVI
495-4844 or (800) 235-4077
FAX 495-4056

Comments: This pretty property features nine one- or two-bed-room villas with full kitchens. There's a small pool and beach and a very relaxing atmosphere. Expensive.

Heritage Villas
PO Box 1019, Road Town
Tortola, BVI
494-5842

Comments: Located up on Windy Hill, these one- and two-bed-room apartments feature some of the best views in the BVI. Moderate to Expensive.

Long Bay Beach Resort & Villas
c/o PO Box 284
Larchmont, NY 10538
(914) 833-3318 or (800) 729-9599
FAX (914) 833-3318

Comments: Set on one of the best beaches in the BVI, the pretty property features 70 rooms and villas in a wide array of styles and prices. Elegant dining and amenities make this a special place to stay on Tortola. Expensive.

Maria's By the Sea
PO Box 206, Road Town
Tortola, BVI
494-2595
FAX 494-2420

Comments: This Road Town inn is a BVI bargain. The simple rooms all offer kitchenettes and balconies. Friendly people and a great location make this an ideal budget choice. Inexpensive.

Moorings - Mariner Inn
PO Box 139, Road Town
Tortola, BVI
494-2332 or (800) 535-7289

Comments: For the sailing set, this is a popular place to stay as a break from the boat. Divers will also like the location and the atmosphere. The large Mooring Charter sailboat firm is based here, drawing all sorts of characters from throughout the Caribbean. The simple rooms and amenities, combined with a closeness to Road Town, make the Mariner Inn a solid choice. Moderate to Expensive.

Nanny Cay Resort and Marina
PO Box 281, Road Town
Tortola, BVI
494-1512 or (800) 74-CHARMS (reservations)
FAX 494-3288

Comments: Major renovations have made this water-oriented hotel a good choice. Small buildings are situated around gardens and pools. The sailing set make for an interesting atmosphere. Moderate to Expensive.

Ole Works Inn
Cane Garden Bay
Tortola, BVI
495-4837; FAX 495-9618

Comments: This quaint inn, owned by Tortola musician Quito Rhymer, is situated above a beautiful beach. Simple amenities and friendly people. Inexpensive.

Prospect Reef Resort
PO Box 104, Road Town
Tortola, BVI
494-3311, (800) 356-8937 (U.S.),
or (800) 453-3608 (Canada)
FAX 494-5595

Comments: This large resort is one of Tortola's best choices. The accommodations and amenities are first class, with a wide choice of rooms (ranging from small economy rooms to large two-bedroom apartments). A Baskin In The Sun operation is conveniently located next to the harbor right on the hotel's property and many hotel/dive packages are available. Expensive.

Rhymer's Beach Hotel
Box 570, Cane Garden Bay
Tortola, BVI
495-4639

Comments: Situated right on Cane Garden Bay, the highlight of this hotel is the beautiful beach. Accommodations are simple, but do include small kitchenettes. This is a sound budget choice on the beach. Inexpensive to Moderate.

Sea Breeze Vacations
PO Box 528, East End
Tortola, BVI
494-2483

Comments: This well-run company offers an extensive range of condominium and house rentals throughout Tortola, providing a unique way to live among the locals.

Sugar Mill Hotel
Box 425, Road Town
Tortola, BVI
495-4355 or (800) 462-8834
FAX 495-4696

Comments: Jinx and Jefferson Morgan, well-known writers, own this attractive but small hotel. The rooms are clean and simple, while the atmosphere is pure Caribbean. Their popular restaurant is located in an old sugar mill. This hillside choice is ideal for divers looking for something different. Expensive.

Treasure Isle Hotel
PO Box 68, Road Town
Tortola, BVI
494-2501

Comments: This is another Moorings hotel. It is located on a hillside overlooking the harbor and town. The pretty property features large rooms and basic amenities. Moderate to Expensive.

Village Cay Resort Marina and Hotel
PO Box 145, Road Town
Tortola, BVI
494-2771; FAX 494-2773

Comments: Like the Mariner Inn, sailors love Village Cay Resort Marina and Hotel. It's small, friendly, and close to Road Town. Moderate.

Virgin Gorda

Biras Creek Estate
PO Box 54
Virgin Gorda, BVI
494-3555/6
FAX 494-3557

Comments: If you want to get away from it all, try Biras Creek. This secluded piece of paradise is only reached by boat. The 150-acre resort is beyond comparison in the Caribbean, with an elegant setting and beautiful guest cottages. The dining, views, and amenities make this a first-class choice. Expensive.

Bitter End Yacht Club & Resort
PO Box 46, North Sound
Virgin Gorda, BVI
494-2746

In the U.S., contact officials of Bitter End at:

875 N. Michigan Avenue
Chicago, IL 60611
(312) 944-5855 or (800) 872-2392
FAX (312) 944-2860

Comments: If you love being surrounded by the sailing set, Bitter End is the legendary place to stay in the BVI. A selection of accommodations (including boats), a casual atmosphere, and very friendly staff draws many repeat visitors to Bitter End. If you've always wanted to learn how to sail, this is the place to do it. If you've dreamed of easy BVI diving, Kilbride's Underwater Tours right on site can make it happen. They offer flexible packages for divers and other activity-minded guests. Expensive.

Fischer's Cove Beach Hotel
Box 60, The Valley
Virgin Gorda, BVI
495-5252

Comments: This quaint little property is simple and relatively inexpensive, boasting a nice beach and a casual feeling. Moderate.

Guavaberry Spring Bay
PO Box 20
Virgin Gorda, BVI
495-5227

Comments: The treehouse-style one- and two-bedroom cottages, sitting on stilts, make Guavaberry Spring Bay a unique choice. The location, overlooking a beautiful beach and near The Baths, is ideal. Moderate to Expensive.

Leverick Bay Hotel
PO Box 63, The Valley
Virgin Gorda, BVI
495-7421 or (800) 848-7081 (U.S.)
(800) 463-9396 (Canada)

Comments: Leverick Bay is booming and this is a great place to stay if you want to be in the center of it all. There is nearby diving with Dive B.V.I. The rooms, perched on a hill overlooking the harbor, have a fresh feel to them and offer great views. Further up, you can opt for two-bedroom condominiums. Moderate to Expensive.

Little Dix Bay
PO Box 70
Virgin Gorda, BVI
495-5555 or (800) 223-7637 (reservations)
FAX 495-5661

Comments: The sister resort of St. John's elegant Caneel Bay, Little Dix Bay is every bit as good. Why not stay at both? A recent refurbishment program has made Little Dix Bay better than ever. This resort features wonderful rooms, superior service, a beautiful beach, every amenity imaginable, and elegant dining. It makes for a very special stay. Expensive.

Mango Bay Resort
PO Box 1062
Virgin Gorda, BVI
495-5672/3
FAX 495-5674

Comments: This is truly a get-away-from-it-all BVI resort. There are only eight villas situated on a quiet beach. Expensive.

Olde Yard Inn
PO Box 26
Virgin Gorda, BVI
495-5544; FAX 495-5986

Comments: The Olde Yard Inn is owned and run by Carol Kaufman and Charlie Williams who take special pride in their wonderful establishment. Located outside Spanish Town in the Virgin Gorda countryside, this inn draws rave reviews from guests for the personal service, pleasant rooms, quiet atmosphere, and new pool. Moderate.

Paradise Beach Resort
Mahoe Bay
Virgin Gorda, BVI
495-5871 or (800) 225-4255

Comments: Another out-of-the way option, this is truly a paradise in the BVI. Guests have a choice of one-, two-, or three-bedroom units overlooking the beach. For BVI explorers, Paradise Beach Resort includes a jeep rental during your stay. Expensive.

Tula's N&N Campground
Little Harbour
Virgin Gorda, BVI
774-0774

Comments: Tula's is definitely the best budget choice on Virgin Gorda. They have bare sites for completely outfitted campers, as well as prepared sites for those have not brought everything along with them. Inexpensive.

Anegada

Anegada Reef Hotel
Anegada, BVI
495-8002
FAX 495-9392

Comments: Located 20 miles north of Virgin Gorda, Anegada's landscape is completely different from the rest of the BVI chain. The volcanic island is virtually flat and is home to fewer than 200 people, including the guests of the Anegada Reef Hotel. This small resort is a complete escape, with simple accommodations, beaches, cooking, and amenities. It has a loyal following of repeat guests. Expensive.

Cooper Island

Cooper Island Beach Club
PO Box 859, Road Town
Tortola, BVI
494-3732

Comments: Like Anegada, Cooper Island is a complete escape. The small resort offers four units, all with kitchens and balconies. Although there's been a popular restaurant on the island for many years, the guest rooms were built only in 1992. It's a quiet resort that is a popular stopover point with the boating set. Try to stay longer if you can. Underwater Safaris has a great operation right on the property. Moderate.

Guana Island

Guana Island Club
PO Box 32, Road Town
Tortola, BVI
(914) 967-6050 or (800) 544-8262
FAX (914) 967-8048

Comments: Another ultra-secluded BVI resort (and island), Guana Island and Guana Island Club are reached only by the resort's boat from nearby Tortola. Once there, this private island features simple accommodations on a hill overlooking the beach and the bright blue Caribbean. If you want a completely private getaway, this may be it. Expensive.

Jost Van Dyke

Rudy's Mariner Inn
Great Harbour
Jost Van Dyke, BVI
495-9282
FAX 775-3558 (USVI)

Comments: This simple inn is a great budget choice on Jost Van Dyke, a beautiful island that is well worth visiting for its restaurants (see below) and laid-back atmosphere. Inexpensive.

Sandcastle
White Bay
Jost Van Dyke, BVI
771-1611 or 495-9282 (USVI)
FAX 775-3590 (USVI)

Comments: This small cottage enclave is as quiet as the rest of Jost Van Dyke. The friendly and casual atmosphere has a loyal following. Moderate.

Marina Cay

Marina Cay
PO Box 76, Road Town
Tortola, BVI
494-2174
FAX 494-4775

Comments: This tiny island just off Tortola has a few villas for rent. Marina Cay offers a good value for those in search of privacy. Moderate.

Mosquito Island

Drake's Anchorage Resort Inn
PO Box 2510, North Sound
Virgin Gorda, BVI
494-2254
FAX 494-2254

Comments: Located just across the water from Virgin Gorda, Mosquito Island and Drake's Anchorage feature BVI seclusion at its best. The quiet and simple atmosphere here is enhanced by lots of hammocks and an excellent restaurant (see below). Along with basic rooms, Drake's Anchorage also offers suites and villas. Expensive.

Peter Island

Peter Island Resort
PO Box 211, Road Town
Tortola, BVI
494-2561/2
FAX 494-2313

Comments: Located five miles south of Tortola, Peter Island is a secluded island with a resort to match the surroundings. The rooms, dining (see below), services, and amenities are all first class, making it one of the top resorts in the entire Caribbean. There's a dive shop on site and a wide array of other outdoor activities. Expensive.

Dining

Like a BVI vacation, dining can be almost anything you want it to be. You will find almost every cuisine and atmosphere imaginable.

Dining in the BVI is not cheap. The restaurant listings given below are rated as follows:

> Inexpensive: less than $15 per person
> Moderate: between $15 and $30 per person
> Expensive: more than $30 per person

Tortola

The Apple, Little Apple Bay, 495-4437. If you're searching for a place where you can taste the local cuisine in an elegant, yet casual atmosphere, this restaurant will be the apple of your eye. Seafood and local cooking are the meals of choice, including a huge barbecue and buffet on Sundays. Moderate.

Brandywine Bay, Sir Francis Drake Highway, 495-2301. One of the top restaurants in the BVI, Brandywine offers Italian cooking with Caribbean touches at its best. Owner and chef Pugliese produces tasty, creative dishes and serves them at this elegant restaurant, which has outstanding views. Expensive.

The Last Resort, Bellamy Cay, 495-2520. A short ferry ride takes diners to this casual restaurant located on Bellamy Cay. It features a popular British buffet. Moderate.

Mrs. Scatliffe's, Carrot Bay, 495-4556. This family-style establishment features fine local cooking and friendly service. It's the perfect place for a casual evening. Inexpensive.

Pusser's Landing, Soper's Hole, Frenchman's Bay, 495-4554. Part of the popular Pusser's "chain," this one is located at Soper's Hole and is a favorite of sailors. There's a great bar and casual dining downstairs, with a quieter atmosphere upstairs. Moderate.

Pusser's Outpost, Waterfront Drive, south of Road Town, 495-4199. Another popular Pusser's hangout, this bar and restaurant is located above a Pusser's Deli and Company Store. They offer dining indoors and on a balcony, as well as a huge champagne brunch on Sundays. Moderate.

Quito's Gazebo, Cane Garden Bay, 495-4837. Located at the Ole Works Inn (see "Accommodations") and also owned by Quito Rhymer, this local hangout features some of the best seafood in town. The food, atmosphere, and entertainment are pure Caribbean. Inexpensive.

Skyworld, Ridge Road, 494-3567: The views and food make this a spectacular spot for lunch or dinner. Expensive.

Spaghetti Junction, Waterfront Drive, 494-4880. If you have a hankering for pasta, this casual spot is a popular pick. Inexpensive to Moderate.

The Struggling Man, Sea Cow Bay, 494-4163. Local fare and a Caribbean atmosphere, with friendly service and a super view. Inexpensive.

Sugar Mill, Sugar Mill Hotel, Carrot Bay, 495-4355. Jinx and Jeff Morgan run this restaurant at their famed hotel (see above). The quiet atmosphere and elegant food make this a truly special night out. Expensive.

Tavern in the Town, Waterfront Drive, 494-2790. As the name suggests, this tavern is located right in Road Town. The British atmosphere and food are popular. Inexpensive to Moderate.

The Upstairs, Prospect Reef Resort, 494-2228. This elegant Prospect Reef (see above) restaurant offers nice views and superb Continental fare. Expensive.

Virgin Queen, Fleming Street, 494-2310. This a popular Road Town bar and restaurant. It features an assorted menu ranging from their famous pizza to good local cooking. Inexpensive.

Virgin Gorda

The Bath and Turtle, Virgin Gorda Yacht Harbour, 494-2746. This casual establishment is frequented by locals. It is perfect for a quick bite or drink on the outdoor patio. Inexpensive.

Biras Creek, Biras Creek Hotel, 494-3555. For a very special meal (or stay), take a boat to Biras Creek. If you don't have a boat, they'll come and pick you up. This excellent resort also has one of the best restaurants in the BVI. Superior food and wine are served in an elegant, candlelit atmosphere. This is an evening you won't forget. Those who dine at Biras Creek often end up staying there during their next BVI dive trip, which gives you an idea of the impression it makes. Expensive.

The Clubhouse, Bitter End Yacht Club, 494-2746. The Bitter End's restaurant serves great food and cold drinks to hungry and thirsty sailors (and divers). The buffet is especially popular at this well-known resort. Moderate to Expensive.

The Crab Hole, The Valley, 495-5307. If you want local cooking, head to The Valley for a good selection of meals with Caribbean flair and unique island touches. Inexpensive.

Drake's Anchorage, Mosquito Island, 494-2254. Located at the fine resort of the same name on Mosquito Island (see above), this Caribbean-style restaurant is definitely worth a trip. Like Biras Creek, if you go for dinner, you'll want to stay much longer. Expensive.

Little Dix Bay, Little Dix Bay, 495-5555. If you're not staying at Little Dix Bay, be sure to head there for at least one meal. Extensive renovations have made the resort and restaurant even more elegant. Expensive.

Olde Yard Inn, The Valley, 495-5544. This excellent restaurant is housed in a hotel of the same name. The French-inspired menu is worth the drive, as is the warm welcome from Carol Kaufman and Charlie Williams. Moderate.

Pusser's Leverick Bay, Leverick Bay, 495-7369. This "chain" of British-style pubs is the perfect place for a drink or some filling pub grub. Situated right on the water, it's a great hangout. Moderate.

Teacher's Pet Ilma's, The Valley, 495-5355. This is one of the best bets in the BVI for local cooking. The seafood and goat dishes are outstanding. Inexpensive.

Anegada

Anegada Reef Hotel, 495-8002. This wonderful hotel also features a great bar and seafood restaurant. Inexpensive to Moderate.

Pomato Point Inn, Pomato Point, 495-8038. Wilfred Creque is the delightful host at this casual beach restaurant and bar, which is just down from the Anegada Reef Hotel. Inexpensive to Moderate.

Cooper Island

Cooper Island Beach Club, 494-3732. This quiet resort is also popular with the sailing set for food and drink stopovers. Moderate.

Jost Van Dyke

Rudy's Mariner Rendezvous, Great Harbour, 495-9282. This simple local inn is a great budget choice on Jost Van Dyke, a beautiful island that is well worth visiting for its restaurants and laid-back atmosphere. Try the lobster. Inexpensive.

Other excellent choices on Jost Van Dyke include: **Abe's Little Harbour** (no phone); **Club Paradise** (495-9267); **Foxy's Tamarind** (495-9258); and **Sydney's Peace and Love** (495-9271). All are inexpensive, casual, and fun.

Marina Cay

Marina Cay, 494-2174. This tiny island just off Tortola features a small hotel and a very popular restaurant and bar. It's reached by ferry and makes for an enjoyable and tasty outing. Moderate.

Mosquito Island

Drake's Anchorage, 494-2254. Located just across the water from Virgin Gorda, Mosquito Island and Drake's Anchorage both offer seclusion. The quiet atmosphere here is enhanced by lots of hammocks and an excellent Caribbean-style restaurant. It makes for a great outing if you're staying in the BVI. Expensive.

Peter Island

Tradewinds, Peter Island Resort, 494-2561/2. Located about five miles south of Tortola. The dining and atmosphere at Tradewinds are first class, making it one of the top resort restaurants in the BVI and well worth the boat ride. Expensive.

Entertainment

The entertainment and nightlife scene in the BVI is typically subdued. However, you can find what you want if you know where to go.

On Tortola, try **Bomba's Surfside Shack** (no phone), one of the **Pusser's** (see above), or **Quito's Gazebo** (see above). On Virgin Gorda, many resorts and restaurants also feature an active nightlife scene. Some possibilities include **The Bath and Turtle**, **Crab Hole**, and **Pusser's**, all of which are listed above.

On the other islands, the entertainment is usually associated with the resorts or restaurants. Call ahead to see if anything is happening.

Sightseeing

Tortola

Though exploring on your own is easy and pleasurable, small groups may enjoy an island tour with **B.V.I. Taxi Association**, 494-2875; **Scato's Bus Service**, 494-2365; **Style's Taxi Service**, 494-2260; or **Travel Plan Tours**, 494-2872.

Road Town: The BVI capital is just as quiet as the rest of this island nation. Sir Olva Georges Square sits at the center of it all and it's worth visiting, along with Main Street and Waterfront Street. The British Virgin Islands Museum (no phone) is just off the square. Its collection of artifacts salvaged from the wreck of *RMS Rhone* are of interest, particularly to divers. The rest of Road Town features excellent shopping, dining, and lots of friendly locals.

Brewer's Bay: This rugged area features one of the prettiest beaches on Tortola, as well as Mt. Healthy National Park, where explorers can find a beautiful old sugar mill.

Cane Garden Bay: Another great beach, this one is easier to get to than Brewer's Bay and can be a bit more crowded. It's still rarely busy and is a good spot for sunning and a cool dip.

Long Bay: On an island of great beaches, this mile-long strip is one of the best. If you're not staying on or near Long Bay (see above), this attractive, pristine spot makes for a great day at the beach.

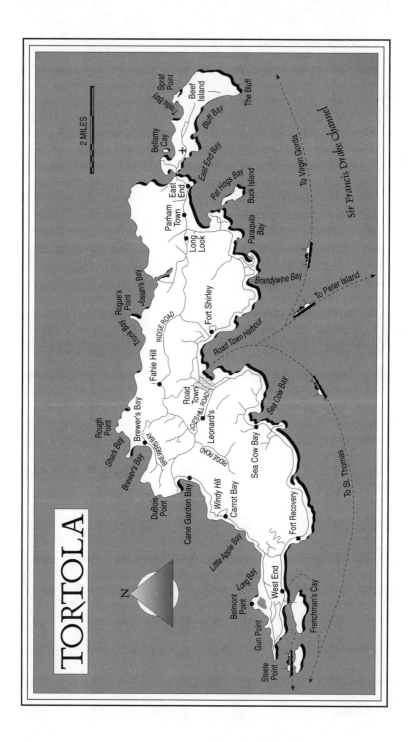

TORTOLA

N

2 MILES

Sprat Point
The Bluff
Beef Island
Trellis Bay
Bluff Bay
Bellamy Cay
East End Bay
Fat Hogs Bay
East End
Buck Island
Parham Town
Paraquita Bay
Long Look
Brandywine Bay
Josiah's Bay
Rogue's Point
Fort Shirley
To Virgin Gorda
Trunk Bay
RIDGE ROAD
Road Town Harbour
To Peter Island
Fahie Hill
Road Town
Sir Francis Drake Channel
JOE'S HILL ROAD
Rough Point
Brewer's Bay
Leonard's
Sea Cow Bay
Shark Bay
BREWERS BAY
RIDGE ROAD
Brewer's Bay
Sea Cow Bay
DuBois Point
Windy Hill
Cane Garden Bay
Carrot Bay
Sea Cow Bay
Little Apple Bay
Fort Recovery
To St. Thomas
Belmont Point
Long Bay
West End
Gun Point
Frenchman's Cay
Steele Point

Belmont Point: Located at the west end of Long Bay, this steep promontory offers one of the best views (and picture-taking spots) in the BVI.

Frenchman's Cay: This little island is connected to Tortola by a small bridge. Visitors will enjoy the boating community, the locals, the shopping, and the drinking and dining at Pusser's Landing (see above).

Fort Recovery: Located on the road back into Road Town, this small 17th-century fort is worth a quick stop.

Virgin Gorda

For an interesting local tour by taxi, contact **Andy's Taxi Service and Jeep Rental**, 495-5252; **Mahogany Rentals and Taxi Service**, 495-5469; and **Speedy's Taxi Service**, 495-5234.

Spanish Town: This tiny town is the quintessential Caribbean outpost. Part of The Valley, there is little to see in Spanish Town, other than a few shops, boats, and nice locals.

The Baths: Perhaps the most famous site in the BVI, these highly unusual rock formations tower above the water and surrounding landscape. They are more commonly explored on foot or by snorkelers, but diving here can also be quite interesting (see above). No matter how you explore The Baths, try to get there in early morning or late afternoon to avoid the crowds.

Copper Mine Point: This old copper mine was built by Spanish settlers more than 400 years ago and is one of the few historic sightseeing stops on Virgin Gorda.

Black Rock: This promontory at a narrow part of the island provides great views to the sea and of the rest of Virgin Gorda.

Gorda Peak: Part of the Gorda Peak National Park, the highest point on the island is reached by a short, steep hike to a platform for some stunning views.

Saba Rock: This little island in the middle of Eustatia Sound is the home of BVI diving legend Bert Kilbride. No visit to Virgin

Gorda is complete without a visit to his Pirates Pub and Grill, a Caribbean diving and drinking mecca.

Bitter End Yacht Club and Marina: Even if you're not staying at Bitter End, be sure to stop by Bitter End Yacht Club for a meal or drink. This popular resort is a favorite with the sailing set and has many repeat guests.

Biras Creek: As with Bitter End, visit Biras Creek even if you're not staying there. They have some of the best views and meals in the BVI.

Mosquito Island: Though a separate island, it's connected to Virgin Gorda by frequent boat service. Be sure to head here for a day of exploration, a meal, or a night or more at Drake's Anchorage (see above).

Little Dix Bay: The home to the famed resort by the same name (see above), Little Dix is one of Virgin Gorda's claims to fame. As with Caneel Bay over on St. John, legendary Little Dix Bay was developed by Laurence Rockefeller. If you can't afford to stay here, be sure to stop by for a quick look or a meal.

Anegada

Besides the spectacular and generally unknown diving, there's not too much to see on Anegada. However, the low-lying island has nice accommodations and dining options, as well as some excellent local pottery at **Pat's Pottery**, 495-8031, in the middle of the island.

Cooper Island

The sightseeing attraction on Cooper Island is the **Cooper Island Beach Club** and it's well worth a visit for rubbing elbows with the transient sailing community.

Jost Van Dyke

Even if you're not staying on this quiet island, consider visiting for a great meal and a quick tour (the tiny enclave of Great Harbour is a classic Caribbean town).

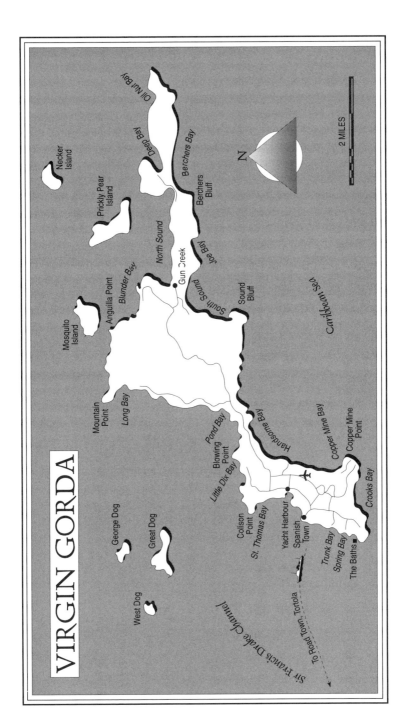

VIRGIN GORDA

Oil Nut Bay

Deep Bay

Necker Island

Prickly Pear Island

Berchers Bay

Berchers Bluff

N

2 MILES

Mosquito Island

North Sound

Gun Creek

Joe Bay

South Sound

Sound Bluff

Caribbean Sea

Anguilla Point

Blunder Bay

Mountain Point

Long Bay

Pond Bay

Blowing Point

Handsome Bay

Copper Mine Bay

Copper Mine Point

George Dog

Great Dog

Little Dix Bay

Collson Point

St. Thomas Bay

Yacht Harbour

Spanish Town

Trunk Bay

Spring Bay

The Baths

Crooks Bay

West Dog

Sir Francis Drake Channel

To Road Town, Tortola

Marina Cay

Visitors generally ferry out to Marina Cay for a meal or for one or more nights at the popular restaurant and small hotel of the same name (see above).

Mosquito Island

See information about Mosquito Island and Drake's Anchorage under Virgin Gorda.

Peter Island

As with Cooper Island, the sightseeing attraction on Peter Island is the namesake resort where you are sure to meet interesting characters from around the globe. This hilly island also features many other great views and beaches.

Other Activities

One of the many beauties of a BVI dive vacation is the variety of things to pursue when you're not diving. From watersports to hiking, there is plenty to do.

Beaches

The north side of Tortola has some of the finest beaches in the Caribbean. The best options are Apple Bay, Brewer's Bay, Cane Garden Bay, Long Bay, and Smuggler's Cove at Belmont Bay.

Over on Virgin Gorda, the extensive choices include The Baths, Leverick Bay, Long Bay, Savannah Bay, and Spring Bay. All of the other islands also feature one or more spectacular beaches which are often associated with a resort.

Boating

The beautiful blue Caribbean plays host to a large number of boats and it's an easy task to reserve a boat for an hour, a week, or a month.

Along with the live-aboard options mentioned above, many companies can arrange a charter boat vacation. Some of the best contacts include **Bitter End Yacht Club**, (800) 872-2392 (see "Accommodations"); **Caribbean Connections**, 494-3623; **Catamaran Charters**, (800) 262-0308; **Conch Charters**, (800) 521-8939; **Euphoric Cruises**, (809) 495-5542; **Misty Isle**, 495-5643; **The Moorings**, (800) 535-7289 (see "Accommodations"); **North South**, (800) 387-4964; **Offshore Sail & Motor**, (800) 582-0175; **Sunsail**, (800) 327-2276; **Tortola Marine Management**, (800) 356-8938; and **Tropic Island Management**, (800) 356-8938.

Fishing

For those who enjoy casting a line to catch "The Big One," there are plenty of chances. Deep-sea fishing is quite popular in the BVI. On Tortola, contact **Charter Fishing Virgin Islands** at 494-3311. On Virgin Gorda, contact **Captain Dale on Classic** at Biras Creek, 495-7248.

Horseback Riding

The pretty hills of Tortola are ideal for the equestrian set. Contact **Shadow Stables** at 494-2262 for a spectacular ride suited to your tastes and abilities.

Parasailing

If you want a unique view of the BVI, try parasailing. Many resorts on Tortola and Virgin Gorda offer the opportunity.

Shopping

Though not known for shopping like the USVI, it's still easy and enjoyable to find something to take home as a BVI memory. Most of the shops tend to be small and full of local flavor. Regional art is always a good choice.

On Tortola, the best bet is on and around Road Town or out at Soper's Hole. On Virgin Gorda, try the small shops in Spanish Town. Elsewhere, the various island resorts have shops and can also recommend any local favorites (like Pat's Potter, 495-8031, on Anegada).

Snorkeling

Great diving often means great snorkeling and the BVI offer a number of great sites for those who just can't keep above water during surface intervals and days of flying. Some of the best snorkeling sites include **Long Bay** and **Soper's Hole** on Tortola; **The Baths** and **North Sound** on Virgin Gorda; **White Bay** and **Great Harbour** on Jost Van Dyke; and the **wreck of the** *RMS Rhone* (see above).

Tennis

Most of the tennis courts are located at resorts, but they often let non-guests play for a fee. If you're as serious about tennis as you are about diving, stay at **Little Dix Bay** and enjoy the excellent tennis facilities run by Peter Burwash International (495-5555).

Windsurfing

Many major resorts offer windsurfing lessons and rentals. On Tortola, contact **Boardsailing B.V.I.** at 495-2447. On Virgin Gorda, the place to head is **Bitter End**, (800) 872-2392.

United States Virgin Islands

*T*he U.S. Virgin Islands (USVI) have everything. If you want one of the most popular tourist destinations in the Caribbean, head to St. Thomas. If you want it quiet and natural, stay on St. John. If you want a little bit of both, go to St. Croix. Why not visit and dive all three? You can't go wrong.

The USVI are the Caribbean at its prettiest and most rewarding. It's easy to get to the USVI, with few, if any, travel visas needed, and it's simple to move around between the islands themselves. This archipelago has tourism down to a science and Mother Nature has gifted the USVI with everything from preserved lush mountainous views to desert-like landscapes. A wide variety of diving and lots to do on land make the USVI one of the Caribbean's top dive travel destinations.

History

The history of the USVI is a colorful cultural blend. The islands were inhabited by people long before Columbus "discovered" the islands in 1493. He found the shape of the islands to his liking and named them the Virgin Islands, after Ursula and her 11,000 virgins.

Archaeological research reveals that Indians migrated north in canoes from South America and lived on the islands as early as 710 BC. The islands supported a small population of Arawak

Indians around AD 300 until Carib Indians pursued and enslaved the Arawaks. Columbus skirmished with the Caribs off St. Croix in 1493, but found St. John and St. Thomas uninhabited.

In 1650, the English on St. Croix were ousted by the Spanish, who were driven off by the French that same year. In 1653, St. Croix was ceded to the Knights of Malta, and was later sold to the French.

No lasting settlements were in place until the 1720s. Lucrative sugar cane cultivation convinced the Danes to take formal possession of St. John and St. Thomas. They raised Danish colors in 1718 and thereby established the first permanent European settlement in the islands.

The rich trade attracted many pirates, including Blackbeard and Captain Kidd. They attacked hundreds of ships carrying goods and treasure.

Denmark purchased St. Croix in 1733 and the Virgin Islands stayed under Danish rule for many years. By that same year, virtually all land on St. John was taken up by 109 cane and cotton plantations. The plantations had hundreds of slaves from West Africa, many of whom were tribal nobility and former slave owners themselves. They revolted in 1733, leading to a bloody islandwide massacre of many families.

The 1848 emancipation of slaves was one of many factors leading to the decline of the plantation economy. The population dropped dramatically and by the early 20th century subsistence farming, cattle, and bay rum production had taken over as the main industries.

The U.S. purchased the islands in 1917 and tourism started in earnest in the 1930s. St. Thomas saw rapid development, while St. Croix and St. John have developed more slowly.

Geography

St. Croix is the largest of the USVI, covering 82 square miles. It is located approximately 1,500 miles south/southeast of New

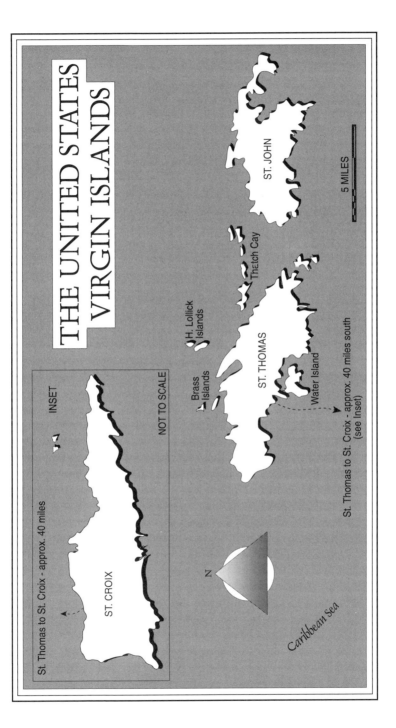

THE UNITED STATES VIRGIN ISLANDS

INSET

St. Thomas to St. Croix - approx. 40 miles

ST. CROIX

NOT TO SCALE

Brass Islands

H. Lollick Islands

ST. THOMAS

Thatch Cay

ST. JOHN

Water Island

St. Thomas to St. Croix - approx. 40 miles south (see Inset)

N

Caribbean Sea

5 MILES

York City and 1,100 miles east/southeast of Miami. The eastern tip of St. Croix is the easternmost Atlantic point in the U.S.

One of St. Croix's most admired geographic features is Buck Island Reef National Monument (see "Sightseeing"). The park features more than 700 acres of clear Caribbean waters and 180 acres of tropical greenery. Visitors can enjoy a hiking trail, an observation tower, and an incredible marked underwater trail.

When Laurence Rockefeller transferred a major part of his St. John real estate holdings to the U.S. government in 1956, he created an untouched and unspoiled American paradise in the Caribbean for all to enjoy. St. John is a little jewel for lovers of the outdoors. Above and below sea level, this island is a 28-square-mile geographic wonder.

St. Thomas covers 33 square miles and offers everything from the urban capital of Charlotte Amalie to green rolling hills.

Tourism Offices

For basic information and informative brochures, call (800) USVI-INFO. For more detailed information and advice, contact the office of the U.S. Virgin Islands Division of Tourism Office nearest you:

225 Peachtree St. N.E., Ste. 760
Atlanta, GA 30303
(404) 688-0906

500 N. Michigan Ave., Ste. 2030
Chicago, IL 60611
(312) 670-8784

3460 Wilshire Blvd., Ste. 412
Los Angeles, CA 90010
(213) 739-0138

2655 Le Jeune Rd., Ste. 907
Coral Gables, FL 33134
(305) 442-7200

1270 Ave. of the Americas, Ste. 2108
New York, NY 10010
(212) 332-2222

900 17th St. N.W., Ste. 500
Washington, DC 20006
(202) 293-3707

1300 Ashford Ave.
Condado, Santurce
Puerto Rico, 00907
724-3816

PO Box 4538
Christiansted
St. Croix, USVI 00840
773-0495

Custom House Bldg., Strand St.
Frederiksted
St. Croix, USVI 00840
772-0357

PO Box 200
Cruz Bay
St. John, USVI 00830
776-6450

PO Box 6400
Charlotte Amalie
St. Thomas, USVI 00804

33 Niagara St.
Toronto, M5V 1C2
Canada
(415) 362-8784

Getting There

By Air

The USVI are among the easiest islands in the Caribbean to
reach. Many of the airlines and tour operators offer a selection
of money-saving packages, which include airfare, accommoda-

tions, and even dives. Airlines change their service often, so it's best to check all options and scout around for the lowest rate.

American Airlines, (800) 433-7300: Nonstop service is currently offered between Miami, New York City, and Raleigh-Durham and St. Thomas. Convenient connecting flights for St. Thomas/St. Croix are also available through San Juan, Puerto Rico, which has turned into a Caribbean airline hub.

Continental Airlines, (800) 231-0856: Nonstop service to St. Thomas.

Delta Airlines, (800) 221-1212: Nonstop service from Newark to St. Thomas, continuing on to St. Croix.

USAir, (800) 428-4322: Nonstop service from Baltimore to St. Thomas, as well as nonstop service from Baltimore, Charlotte, and Philadelphia to San Juan, with connecting service through other airlines.

By Sea

St. Thomas' Charlotte Amalie is one of the world's top boating destinations. It's the Caribbean's most popular cruise ship port (many cruise ship passengers dive the USVI) and is also the base for the Western Hemisphere's largest charter yacht league. In recent years, St. Croix has also seen more cruise ships and yachts. To cater to these additional visitors, many operators run dives for cruise ship passengers as well as for those on other boats.

Entry/Departure Regulations

Because the USVI is a U.S. territory, it's easy for U.S. citizens to enter and leave the islands. Some form of identification is required, such as a driver's license, voter's card, or birth certificate; a U.S. passport is always best. If you plan to travel outside the USVI, you must have a birth certificate or passport. Citizens of other countries should follow whatever the U.S. requires for their country. There are no special health restrictions for those entering from the mainland U.S. or Puerto Rico.

The USVI have become a popular shopping destination because there are no customs duties on tourism-related items (e.g., watches, cameras, jewelry, china, and much more). There is also no luxury or sales tax added.

U.S. residents are allowed a duty-free shopping quota of $1,200, which is twice that of any other island in the Caribbean and three times that of Europe. A flat rate of 5% is charged on any purchases over the $1,200 limit, up to a maximum of $1,000 more. U.S. citizens can also take back up to five cartons of duty-free cigarettes and those 21 years or older can take one gallon of liquor (five fifths), plus an extra fifth if it's a USVI product, such as rum. U.S. residents can also mail an unlimited number of gifts to friends (other than perfume, liquor, and tobacco), each worth $100 or less.

Getting Around

By Air

Air travel between St. Thomas/St. John and St. Croix is easy. It's only a 20-minute flight between St. Thomas and St. Croix. There are flights from both of these to many other Caribbean islands (including the BVI). Airlines servicing the region include **Air Anguilla** (St. Kitts, Nevis, and Anguilla), (809) 776-5789; **Air St. Thomas** (San Juan, St. Barth, and Virgin Gorda), (809) 776-2722; **American Eagle** (service between St. Thomas and St. Croix); **Coastal Air Transport** (Nevis, St. Barth, and Anguilla), (809) 773-6862; **Four Star Aviation** (Virgin Gorda and Beef Island), (809) 777-9900; **Leeward Island Air Transport - LIAT** (service to many Caribbean islands to the south), (809) 462-0701; **SunAir Express** (service betwëen St. Thomas and St. Croix, as well as to San Juan and Tortola); **Windward Island Airways** (Tortola, St. Maarten, St. Kitts, Nevis, and the French West Indies), (809) 775-0183. These small airlines change their service often, so it's best to check with them directly.

By Sea

St. John is only 20 minutes away from Red Hook, St. Thomas by frequent ferry. There is also ferry service from Charlotte Amalie to St. John, which takes about 45 minutes. Contact **Native Son** at 774-8685 or **Smiths Ferry** at 775-7292. The new ferry service between St. Thomas and St. Croix, 773-3900, offers another option for those heading to St. Croix. Called **Surf Express**, the inter-island ferry service between downtown Christiansted and Charlotte Amalie takes about one hour and 15 minutes. Ferry service with **Sundance**, 776-6597, is also offered between St. Thomas and Tortola and Virgin Gorda in the BVI.

By Car

Renting a car is highly recommended on all three islands as long as you have a valid driver's license. This offers the most flexible means of transportation and often leads to more interesting excursion possibilities. Just remember that, as a remnant of Danish rule, traffic drives on the left.

Recommended car rental agencies on St. Croix include **Avis**, 778-9355; **Budget**, 778-9638; **Caribbean Jeep & Car**, 773-4399; **Hertz**, 778-1402; and **Thrifty**, 773-7200. You can rent cars on St. John from **Avis**, 776-6374; **Budget**, 776-7575; **O'Connor Jeep**, 776-6343; **St. John Car Rental**, 776-6103; or **Spencer's Jeep**, 776-7784. On St. Thomas, try **ABC Rentals**, 776-1222 or (800) 524-2080; **Avis**, 774-1468; **Budget**, 778-9638; **Hertz**, 774-1879; and **Thrifty**, 776-7200.

By Bus

Bus service is available on St. Croix and St. Thomas. St. Croix service runs between Christiansted and Frederiksted, while St. Thomas service runs throughout Charlotte Amalie and between Charlotte Amalie, Red Hook and Bordeaux. St. John doesn't have bus service, but taxis and jeeps are available for hire and can be a fun way to explore.

By Taxi

All three islands offer excellent taxi service. Taxi rates are generally based on destination, rather than mileage, and are determined by the government. Confirm the rate before you get in the taxi. Drivers usually pick up additional passengers heading in the same direction. Many taxi drivers also offer excellent tours and will negotiate the price with passengers. The size and quality of taxis can vary greatly. If you have any problems on St. Thomas, contact the **V.I. Taxi Commission** at 776-8294.

Calendar of Events/Holidays

JANUARY	Martin Luther King Day
APRIL	St. Croix's International Triathlon, (800) CALL USVI Rolex Cup Regatta, (800) CALL USVI St. Thomas Carnival, (800) CALL USVI
MAY	Sportfishing tournaments, (800) CALL USVI
JUNE	Organic Act Day
JULY	St. John Carnival, (800) CALL USVI Bastille Day VI Open Atlantic Blue Marlin Tournament (800) CALL USVI
AUGUST	Texas Society Chili Cook-Off, (800) CALL USVI
OCTOBER	Columbus Day/VI-Puerto Rico Friendship Day (800) CALL USVI Hurricane Thanksgiving Day
NOVEMBER	Liberty Day St. Croix Regatta, (800) CALL USVI St. John Coral Bay Regatta, (800) CALL USVI
DECEMBER	St. Croix Christmas Festival

Mail

U.S. Postal Service covers the USVI with similar rates and service to what you would find at home. First-class mail automatically travels by air. Airmail is highly recommended for service between the USVI and other parts of the world. You can reach **FedEx** by calling 774-3393.

Telephone

There is excellent service between the USVI (area code 809) and the rest of the world, including toll-free service (1-800 numbers). Unless otherwise noted, all numbers given are reached through the (809) area code from outside the USVI.

Reading

Any vacation can be enhanced by background reading before and during a trip. For a humorous look at Caribbean life, there's nothing better than Herman Wouk's *Don't Stop the Carnival*. For USVI background, find a copy of *The Three Quarters of the Town of Charlotte Amalie*, by Edith Woods. Harry S. Pariser's *Adventure Guide to the Virgin Islands* gives extensive detail on history, politics and culture found throughout the islands. Local newspapers in the USVI include the *Virgin Islands Daily News*, the *St. Croix Avis*, and *Tradewinds*.

Health

For health emergencies, call the police at 915 or contact individual hospitals. On St. Croix, call the **hospital** at 778-6311. On St. John call the **Cruz Bay Clinic** at 776-6400 or 776-6222 (direct emergency line). On St. Thomas, call the **hospital** at 776-8311. For information regarding companies specializing in dive travel insurance, see "Travel Insurance" in the Introduction.

Diving

Diving in the USVI is special. Though not as well known as other Caribbean or worldwide diving destinations, the diving can be as good and as interesting as anywhere in the world. Diverse diving and many topside attractions make the USVI one of the best spots for smart dive travelers.

Diving conditions are typically ideal for all experience levels, with warm water, calm seas, and excellent visibility. Many of the reefs and wrecks of the USVI are relatively shallow.

All operators will require presentation of your C-card, while some may require a review of your logbook or check-out dive. As with most destinations, a PADI C-card is the most-recognized, but many others are accepted. The USVI also offer a great place to complete your certification process, including entire courses or check-out dives.

St. Thomas offers the only recompression chamber.

Dive Operators

USVI dive operators love their job and get great pleasure in sharing the best dive spots off St. Croix, St. John, and St. Thomas. All are friendly toward visiting divers and do their best to make your trip an unforgettable one.

With so many excellent operators, it's easy to choose one or more companies for their convenience, offerings, and style. Package deals (including diving, accommodations, dining, and more) can make per-dive costs much lower. One of the beauties of all three islands is that a good dive shop and boat is never far away. You may want to try diving with a selection of operators and then purchase a package deal with your personal favorite.

St. Croix

Anchor Dive Center
Salt River Marina
PO Box 5588 S.I.
St. Croix, VI 00823
778-1522
FAX 773-8634

Comments: Because of its unique location at Salt River National Park and Ecological Preserve, Anchor Dive Center offers daily boat access to the northwest shore of St. Croix, where divers find the greatest concentration of dense healthy reefs and walls. Anchor Dive Center guarantees at least one of the "Seven Wonders" (see "Dive Sites") every day. Night dives are available several nights a week and on request. Gear rental and storage is also offered.

Anchor Dive Center dive leaders are knowledgeable about the underwater environment and have a desire to share their understanding of this precious natural habitat. They also have a willingness to helpall divers improve their skills. These enthusiastic individuals share each and every dive, above and below the water, becoming not only reliable dive buddies, but also key contributors to the overall success of each diver's vacation. Less experienced divers can join the tour being offered by the in-water dive instructor.

Blue Dolphin Divers
Route 1, Box 6107, Kings Hill
St. Croix, VI 00823
773-8634
FAX 773-8634

Comments: Typical of many St. Croix dive operators, Blue Dolphin provides a wide variety of flexible dive trips throughout the North Shore.

Cane Bay Dive Shop
Plots 51B & 51C, Estate La Vallée
St. Croix, VI 00824
773-9913
FAX 778-5442

Comments: This unique little shop offers a perfect Cane Bay location and great diving directly off the North Shore. Owners Hal and Day Rosbach have created a shore diving haven right on Cane Bay. They are flexible, convenient, and friendly and will help you as little or as much as you want.

Spectacular shore diving on St. Croix's walls is a short swim away. Boat dives can be tailored to your schedule. For shore diving further afield, Cane Bay Dive Shop's flatbed truck can take you there and pick you up. Dive travelers obviously appreciate this flexibility and this company often sees repeat guests.

They also offer hotel/dive packages with several localized establishments that cater to the needs of individual divers. This is, quite simply, a special dive shop.

Opposite: Southern arches of the wreck of the *Rhone*
(Jim Scheiner, Rainbow Visions Photo Center, Tortola)

Above: Snorkeling off Buck Island, St. Croix *(Carol Lee, US Virgin Islands Dept. of Touri*

Opposite: Orange cup coral *(Jim Scheiner, Rainbow Visions Photo Center, Tortola)*

Below: Sea Turtle, BVI *(Darrell Tasman, Clearwater Productions, St. John)*

Above: Vanishing Rocks, Salt Island *(Jim Scheiner, Rainbow Visions Photo Center, Tortola)*
Opposite: Diver and lobster *(Jim Scheiner, Rainbow Visions Photo Center, Tortola)*
Below: Buck Island, St. Croix *(Carol Lee, US Virgin Islands Dept. of Tourism)*

Above: Soper's Hole, West End, Tortola *(Jim Scheiner, Rainbow Visions Photo Center, To*

Below: Moray eel *(Darrell Tasman, Clearwater Productions, St. John)*

ve: Seahorse *(Darrell Tasman, Clearwater Productions, St. John)*

w: Pederson shrimp on spiral anemone *(Jim Scheiner, Rainbow Visions Photo Center, Tortola)*

Cruzan Divers
#12 Strand Street, Frederiksted
St. Croix, VI 00824
773-3701
FAX (205) 372-4331

Comments: This shop is convenient for West End diving and a different kind of St. Croix experience below the water. For those staying in or near Frederiksted, it's ideal.

Dive Experience
PO Box 4254, Christiansted
St. Croix, VI 00820
773-3307
FAX 773-7030

Comments: This busy Christiansted shop offers convenient North Shore diving for those staying in or near town. Owner Michelle Pugh has made this a popular place with a good selection of fun dives.

Their daily boat trips leave every morning for St. Croix's famous walls, coral reefs, and their well-known fish feed at Chez Barge, just outside the harbor. Beach dives and night dives are available on request.

The Chez Barge dive is something no St. Croix diver should miss. Using fresh fish scraps from local restaurants, divers on this trip can enjoy a fish feeding frenzy on a 110' barge in 60'-100' of water. The fish, attracted in large quantities, typically include snappers, horse-eyed jacks, barracudas, queen triggers, parrot fish, and much more. The stars of the show are several enormous green moray eels.

Michelle Pugh was instrumental in creating the reef-saving moorings system for St. Croix, working with a group called Island Conservation Effort. She has since been elected to the board to help coordinate successful projects on other islands.

Dive Experience offers excellent video services through instructor Sam Halverson. They even sell a high quality video that shows some of their favorite locations on St. Croix. It's a great souvenir.

Opposite: The Baths, Virgin Gorda (*USVI Division of Tourism*)

Dive Experience works with a number of hotels and resorts to offer accommodation/dive package deals. They also offer diving packages tailored to the needs of visiting divers.

> **Dive St. Croix**
> 59 Kings Wharf, Christiansted
> St. Croix, VI 00820
> 773-3434
> FAX 773-9411

Comments: Run by the Sperber brothers, Dive St. Croix is currently the only operator that can run dive trips to Buck Island. This friendly in-town company is ideal if you're staying at the King Christian or anywhere nearby.

> **V.I. Divers**
> Pan Am Pavilion, Christiansted
> St. Croix, VI 00820
> 773-6045 or (800) 544-5911
> FAX 778-7004

Comments: Operating on St. Croix since 1971, the popular Christiansted operator is a good choice for those staying in or near the city. Along with the Christiansted location, owners Jimmy and Kathleen Antoine also maintain watersports centers at several resorts.

The popular dive site, Jimmy's Surprise (see below), is named for Jimmy Antoine and he definitely deserves this honor. This dive shop is a St. Croix diving mecca.

They offer boat dives out of Christiansted every morning and afternoon. The staff is local and friendly, making recommendations on restaurants, shopping, or anything else on the island.

V.I. Divers offers a wide range of packages. One of the best is in conjunction with the Hotel Caravelle (see below) just across the street. It's convenient and diver-friendly.

> **The Waves at Cane Bay**
> 112-C Estate Cane Bay, Christiansted
> St. Croix, VI 00851
> 778-1805 or (800) 545-0603
> FAX 778-4945

Comments: This is shore diving heaven. Kevin and Suzanne Ryan play host at this highly-recommended seaside inn and dive center (see "Accommodations" for details). Famed Cane Bay Drop-off is just 100 yards from the shore. The diving is easy, enjoyable, and personalized.

St. John

Coral Bay Watersports
10-19 Estate Carolina, Coral Bay
St. John, VI 00830
776-6850

Comments: Located in the less-visited town of Coral Bay, this small shop is the best way to reach some of the lesser-known dive sites on the east side of the island.

Cruz Bay Watersports
PO Box 252, Cruz Bay
St. John, VI 00830
776-6234
FAX 693-8720

Comments: Marcus and Patty Johnston make this St. John diving mecca one of the best bases for diving off St. John and St. Thomas. They offer two locations in the town of Cruz Bay and also work closely with the Hyatt Regency (they dock all four boats there). Marcus and Patty and their staff are highly service-oriented and will handle all of your equipment from the first time you set it up until you pack it up to go home. Little touches like fresh fruit, complimentary beverages, and free use of wetsuits mean a lot to Marcus, Patty, and their loyal repeat divers.

There are 25 dive sites within a 15-minute boat ride of the Hyatt. Their favorite dives include Stephens Cay, Devers Canyon, Cow & Calf Rocks, Little St. James, Grass Cay, Congo Rock, Carvel Rock, and the General Rogers. Their biggest boat is also used for day-trips to Jost Van Dyke in the BVI, which is an ideal option on your last day. Along with the Hyatt, Cruz Bay Watersports can arrange accommodation/diving packages at other hotels and condominiums.

Low Key Watersports
PO Box 716, Cruz Bay
St. John, VI 00831
693-8999
FAX 776-6042

Comments: Located right on the water in Cruz Bay, Low Key Watersports is a water-lover's paradise. Bob Shinners and Ann Marie Estes play host, with three dive boats. One boat accommodates 14 divers and the other two take six each. The larger boat is used for groups and long-distance dive trips, like the wreck of the *Rhone* and the *WIT Shoal*. Low Key Watersports also offers snorkeling, sea kayaking (including excellent guided tours), para-sailing, sports fishing, and day sailing. In addition, they can arrange "Stay & Play" packages with their favorite resorts, including Gallows Point Suite Resort and Still Waters.

Paradise Aqua Tours
Maho Bay Camps
St. John, VI 00830
776-6226
FAX 776-6504

Comments: For those staying at the popular campground, Harmony, or anywhere on this side of the island, Paradise Aqua is a great operator to use. George Kremer runs his dive shop and watersports center right on the beach at Maho Bay and campground guests and visiting divers love his style.

Their custom dive boat visits many sites, including the *General Rogers* and the wreck of the *Rhone*. They also feature a weekly trip from Maho Bay to St. Thomas' Coral World, with a morning dive, admission to Coral World, and an afternoon snorkel stop. Night dives and snorkeling are also scheduled.

In keeping with the ecological standards set by Stanley Selengut with Maho Bay and Harmony, Paradise Aqua Tours provides educational and conservation tips for visiting divers. Thanks to people like Selengut, St. John and other beautiful spots will remain a paradise.

Paradise Watersports Shop
Caneel Bay Resort
St. John, VI 00830
776-6111
FAX 776-7078

Comments: If you're lucky enough to be staying at famed Caneel Bay or anywhere on this side of the island, this small operator is a perfect choice.

St. John Watersports
Box 70, Cruz Bay
St. John, VI 00830
776-6256

Comments: Located right in Cruz Bay at Mongoose Junction, Stu Brown's dive company offers a selction of diving and watersports options.

St. Thomas

Aqua Action Dive Center
Secret Harbour Beach Resort
St. Thomas, VI 00802-1305
775-6285
FAX 775-1501

Comments: This full-service watersports shop is perfect for Secret Harbour or nearby guests.

Billy Bad Watersports
Nisky Mail Box 471
St. Thomas, VI 00802
774-4356
FAX 774-4356

Comments: Conveniently located at Limnos Marina, Billy Bad Watersports opened in December of 1993. It is owned and operated by William (Billy) Pratt, a USCG captain and PADI Master Instructor. Billy currently operates one six-pack boat, making for more intimate boat diving. Daily transportation is provided at no extra charge. They work in conjunction with many major resorts, providing all diving services and offering an "Introduction to Scuba" program each day and a complimentary "Local Marine Life" slide show every week at each hotel.

They frequently take divers to sites not usually visited by other operators, such as the wreck of the *WIT Shoal*. Other dive operators visit this site during the day, but Billy Bad's is the only company currently offering the wreck as a night dive. Other favorite dives of this people-oriented operator include the Lobster Bowl, Jake's Reef (known only to them), Turtle Reef, Miss Opportunity, Grain Wreck, Kennedy Wreck, and Cow Rock. If you want personalized diving, call Billy.

Chris Sawyer Diving Center
6300 Estate Frydenhoj, Compass Point Marina
St. Thomas, VI 00802
775-7320 or (800) 882-2965

Comments: This well-known company specializes in smaller groups on its 42' boat. They have a dive shop and excellent package deals with the Stouffer Grand Beach Resort, 775-1510, ext. 7850.

Dean Johnson's Caribbean Diving Institute
Buccaneer Mall, Suite 106-208
St. Thomas, VI 00802
775-7610

Comments: Once known as the Joe Vogel Diving Company, this is the oldest operator in the USVI. They offer personalized service and small group diving.

Dive In
PO Box 5664
St. Thomas, VI 00803
775-6100
FAX 775-4024

Comments: Located at Sapphire Beach Resort and Marina, this is a great spot for convenient beach and boat diving. This full-service dive center offers a wide array of packages, making them even more appealing.

Sea Trade (Sea Horse Dive Boats/Dive Shop)
Suite 505, Crown Bay Marina
St. Thomas, VI 00802
774-2001
FAX 775-4024

Comments: Sea Trade was founded by Capt. Jim McManus, who has been operating his Sea Horse Dive Boats in the Virgin Islands since 1971. Sea Horse Dive Shop is located at Crown Bay Marina on the south side of St. Thomas, providing perfect access to many of the best dive sites. The marina is the newest in the Virgin Islands and offers excellent service, restaurants (Tickles Dockside Pub and Barnacle Bill's), marine services, shops (Gourmet Gallery for groceries), and showers.

Capt. McManus and the Sea Horse crew take divers to more than 50 different dive sites. Sea Horse is especially popular with locals and ship crew members, which is always a good sign to visiting divers (don't worry about having to bring your own buddy).

They offer two-tank dives in the morning and afternoon, with specific sites and night dives booked upon request. They are very flexible in choosing sites and, though their dive boat can handle 16 divers, they'll go with as few as three.

Sea Horse offers free transportation on diving days to and from the following nearby (and recommended) hotels: Emerald Beach Resort; Island Beachcomber; Carib Beach Hotel, Admiral's Inn at Villa Olga; Island View Guest House; and Mafolie Hotel.

St. Thomas Diving Club
7147 Bolongo Bay
St. Thomas, VI 00802
776-2381 or (800) LETS DIVE
FAX 777-2332

Comments: Running an extensive dive operation for Bolongo Bay, this fine company offers a complete selection of dive trips. They cater to an array of skill levels for Bolongo Bay guests and others.

The St. Thomas Diving Club has a comprehensive schedule of St. Thomas/St. John diving, but they also offer weekly *RMS Rhone* trips and night dives and charters. Their Bolongo packages offer some of the best dive travel values in the Caribbean.

> **Underwater Safaris**
> Yacht Haven Marina
> 5300 Long Bay Road, Suite 2, Charlotte Amalie
> St. Thomas, VI 00802
> 774-1350
> FAX 774-8733

Comments: Conveniently located at the Ramada Yacht Haven Marina in Charlotte Amalie and at Marriott's Frenchman's Reef, Underwater Safaris specializes in Buck Island diving. They also cater to the cruise ship crowd and, thus, offer a good number of dives. Owner Mel Luff and manager Gene Chowning make sure that all visiting divers have enjoyable, educational, and safe diving. Whether you're staying at the Ramada, Marriott, or elsewhere, this is friendly and convenient St. Thomas diving.

> **Virgin Island Diving Schools & Supplies**
> PO Box 9707
> St. Thomas, VI 00801
> 774-8687
> FAX 774-7368

Comments: This popular dive shop offers dives, training, and equipment.

Live-Aboards

The closeness of St. John and St. Thomas, as well as the BVI, make the Virgin Islands ideal for live-aboard dive vacation experiences. Many boats and operators can offer diving as part of a boating experience, but if you're a dive fanatic, living aboard a boat means you have the option to dive when you want, where you want and as often as you could wish.

> *Club Med 1*
> 7975 N. Hayden Rd.
> Scottsdale, AZ 85258
> (800) 258-2633

Comments: This 191-cabin sailing cruise ship is an excellent way to dive and explore the Caribbean. The seven-day cruise spends three days in the waters of the Virgin Islands (both BVI and USVI). It sails out of Martinique and is a unique scuba diving adventure, with lots of extras. Club Med diving fans will love this option.

> **Irie Dive & Sail Charters**
> 5100 Long Bay Rd, Flagship
> St. Thomas, USVI 00802
> 774-5630
> FAX 776-3074

Comments: *Irie* is the perfect choice for those looking to explore the Virgin Islands. Based in St. Thomas, this 46′ sailing vessel provides a unique diving and sailing vacation in crystal-clear waters.

Irie's crew are excellent dive instructors and know the best dive sites around. The sailing and diving make a great combination.

> **Regency Yacht Vacations**
> 5200 Long Bay Road
> St. Thomas, USVI 00802
> 776-5950 or (800) 524-7676
> FAX 776-7631

Comments: Based in St. Thomas, Regency Yacht Vacations represents hundreds of yachts in the Virgin Islands, many of which offer dive charters. Charter consultant Michon Willman is experienced at working with divers and can help them choose the right boat. The choices include *Irie* (see above), *Whisper* (a 44′ sailing ship owned and captained by Gwen Hamlin), and more. Diving takes place throughout the Virgin Islands.

Photography/Video

Most operators offer a selection of still photography and video options. It's best to call ahead to check on programs, instruction, rentals, and development. Take this opportunity to put on film the spectacular underwater world of the USVI. You can do anything from macro work to wide angle shots. For a special photography experience, contact **Darrell Tasman** on St. John at

693-9071. His company, Clearwater Productions, provides photo/video services to local dive shops and hotels. Darrell's underwater photography from throughout the Caribbean is well known.

Dive Sites

The USVI lie at the edge of a huge underwater shelf that extends some 85 miles from Puerto Rico before dropping off in the Atlantic to the north and the Caribbean to the south. Most of the sport diving in the USVI is on that shelf, where many wrecks and fascinating underwater formations are at a reasonable depth for divers.

The compactness of St. John and St. Thomas, combined with the wall diving on the north side of St. Croix, are big advantages to the diver. The sheltering effect of the islands cuts the wind speed at most sites. Summer and winter temperatures in the USVI are pretty much the same above and below the surface.

The following review of potential dive sites in the USVI should serve only as a guide. Keep in mind that conditions change. The descriptions, depths, and levels of expertise needed are intentionally general and given only as a framework to work from. A local dive operator should always be consulted about the current condition of dive sites.

Preparation is the key to safe and enjoyable diving. Be sure your equipment has been properly serviced and set up. If you haven't been diving recently, consider a refresher course or dive, as well as additional training while you're in the USVI.

Conservation is the key to the future enjoyment of diving in the USVI and elsewhere. Divers should adhere to all accepted and local rules and etiquette for preserving the reef. Take only pictures and leave only bubbles.

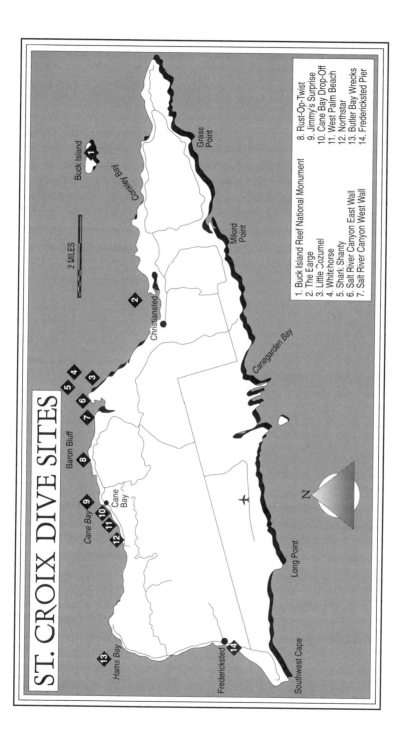

ST. CROIX DIVE SITES

1. Buck Island Reef National Monument
2. The Earge
3. Little Cozumel
4. Whitehorse
5. Shark Shanty
6. Salt River Canyon East Wall
7. Salt River Canyon West Wall
8. Rust-Op-Twist
9. Jimmy's Surprise
10. Cane Bay Drop-Off
11. West Palm Beach
12. Northstar
13. Butler Bay Wrecks
14. Fredericksted Pier

Buck Island

Grass Point

Conkley Bay

2 MILES

Christiansted

Mlord Point

Canegarden Bay

Baron Bluff

Cane Bay

Cane Bay

Hams Bay

Long Point

Fredericksted

Southwest Cape

N

St. Croix

Frank "Sharkey" Vince of Anchor Dive Center loves the "Seven Wonders" dive sites on St. Croix (Salt River Canyon East Wall, Salt River Canyon West Wall, Shark Shanty, Jimmy's Surprise, Cane Bay, Whitehorse, and Northstar). His descriptions, along with summaries of many other dive sites, provide a perfect introduction to diving the island.

"St. Croix's dive sites are certainly thrilling by any Caribbean standard. Their abundance and variety make it possible to dive day after day, always experiencing new and different landscapes. Everything from walls to pinnacles, reefs to wrecks, underwater plateaus, ledges, caverns, and caves are here to explore.

Although most of the sites are suitable for divers of any experience level, there's plenty of action for moderate to advanced divers. Opportunities to make deep pinnacle dives will reward advanced divers with many thrills."

1. Buck Island Reef National Monument (0'-60'; novice to expert): Though this incredible site is known mainly for snorkeling, the diving is also quite spectacular. This 850-acre land and sea park is administered and protected by the National Park Service. Many operators run day-trips to the excellent snorkeling trail and fine beach, but Dive St. Croix is the only dive operator currently allowed to run guided dive trips here. Even with the crowds of snorkelers, the reef is in pretty good shape. You will find easy diving and a fair amount of marine life and underwater caves. During surface intervals, Buck Island's beach is one of the best in the USVI.

2. The Barge (60'-90'; novice to expert): This artificial reef is an old barge that was intentionally sunk close to the channel off Christiansted. It has turned into a popular dive site because of the hundreds of fish that have become accustomed to being fed by divers. The Barge is a great spot for underwater photography.

3. Little Cozumel, (40'-80'; novice to expert): This attractive site features two small walls that run from about 40' down to 70'.

There is abundant and colorful coral growth on the sheer faces, making it an interesting "wall" experience. An undercut at about 65' probes 20' into the wall, where you'll find plenty of growth and many fish.

4. Whitehorse (0'-25'; advanced to expert): Sharkey Vince considers this one of the world's most exciting shallow dives. The average depth at Whitehorse is 12 feet, but don't mistake this for a snorkeling site.

This dramatic dive is a virtual explosion of color and light. The reef itself is deeply scored with large open crevices, a tunnel, and an arch. Inside, divers can seek shelter from the continual surge that comes from waves breaking overhead and get to see a wave from the inside out, while peeking out over the edge of a crevice to avoid being dashed against the rock and coral. Small tropicals hover overhead and are caught up in the typhoon of tumbling waves. They attract large predators like houndfish and barracudas who come to snack on the abundant supply of food.

The jagged point of rock that comes within a few inches of the surface has caused the demise of many ships. Divers can look in the calmer waters around the plateau's perimeter for evidence of shipwrecks, including anchors, cannon, ballast, and anchor chain. They may also count on spotting the rare and elusive sailfin blenny here.

5. Shark Shanty (40'-65'; novice to expert): Somewhat further from shore than a typical St. Croix dive site, this spot is known only to Anchor Dive Center. The area is characterized by a flat-bottomed gorgonian garden that is punctuated by a large football-shaped sandy trench. The ridge and occasional ledges along its perimeter house many rare and beautiful creatures, including saucereye porgies, eagle rays, hawksbill turtles, porkfish, box crabs, conch, chain morays, starfish, queen triggerfish, octopi, hogfish, and much more. This is a unique site.

6. Salt River Canyon East Wall (35'-130'; novice to expert): This thrilling dive is often called "the fishiest dive on the north shore," thanks to the huge schools of yellowtail snappers, durgeons, and creole wrasses that patrol the edge of the wall. More exotic tropicals, such as pork fish, spotted drum, yellow-headed jawfish, and many varieties of angel fish also reside on the East Wall.

The wall is a sponge- and coral-encrusted slope plunging downward from a soft coral garden at about 35'. Lacy sea fans add a decorative touch. A pair of large, curious horse-eye jacks often investigate divers closely at The Point. The wall makes a 90° turn at Barracuda Banks, where many barracudas come to tidy up at numerous cleaning stations.

7. Salt River Canyon West Wall (25'-130'; novice to expert): This steep and rugged wall is the most requested boat dive on St. Croix. The countless pinnacles, ledges, and recesses are comparible to the geologic formations found in the American southwest. Divers will find it exhilarating to swim between numerous pinnacles.

Most divers find themselves enraptured with the cuts and recesses that weave through the wall. Long passages under ledges and between pinnacles appear like engrossing mazes that cause divers to all but forget the outside world. While some pinnacles are small (about the size of a barrel), others are larger than most houses.

Large green morays, barracudas, and lions paw sea cucumbers are commonly found here. There are also lots of black durgeons, grunts, snappers, and creole wrasse that school at the upper edge of the wall just 20 feet below the surface. On occasion, mantas glide in to feed in the plankton-rich waters. This is also a highly noted night dive, where the widest variety of crustaceans march out to join basket stars, octopi, and Barnacle Bill, the massive hawksbill turtle.

8. Rust-Op-Twist (35'-110'; novice to expert): Named for a sugar plantation that was once located on shore nearby, this dive features long pipes that serve as ideal navigational tools. The currents at this spot ensure a wide variety of fish and coral life, as the reef gradually slopes down to a wall at about 110'.

9. Jimmy's Surprise (55'-130'; advanced to expert): Named for former dive guide, Jimmy Antoine, this is the site that attracts the pros. The biggest fish off St. Croix's reefs are most likely to be spotted schooling around this wondrous off-shore sea mount. Horse eye and cralle jacks, sharks, and green morays join the proliferation of common tropicals.

The large pinnacle that is the dive's focus rises up from 95 feet to within 60 feet of the surface. A dense covering of lacy sea fans decorates its western face and many large unusually shaped barrel sponges pepper a wide rocky include on the east side, where big morays are frequently found. A deep crevice at the pinnacle's base sometimes hides groupers, lobsters, or nurse sharks. Some playful gray angels love to follow divers overhead, nipping at their exhaust bubbles. Special sightings might include snake eels, octopi, and eagle rays, while hawksbill turtles are quite common.

Strong currents and surge often make Jimmy's Surprise a challenging dive. The lack of any shallow areas in which to off-load nitrogen further complicates the dive. No wimps, please!

10. Cane Bay Drop-Off (30'-130'; novice to expert): Everyone should dive Cane Bay when they're on St. Croix. Local operators run boat and shore dive excursions to this popular site. Divers drop straight into a lush reef with the largest coral heads on the island. This is one of the few "patch" reefs on St. Croix.

The rich coral mounds are separated by open sand areas. Divers will spot remnants of a little Cessna two-seater that crashed here long ago. Head a little deeper and the corals coalesce into giant ribs separated by deep wide sand trenches.

Swim east parallel to shore and you'll come upon some unusual tall formations jutting up from the reef. The fish population is quite dense in this area, with unusual creatures including chubs, reef sharks, seahorses, and Atlantic spadefish.

A little further along, you reach a deep funnel of sand beckoning you to greater depths. Follow this one down to about 70 feet and you'll suddenly spy the first of three ancient anchors lost here during the days of slave trade and sugar cane plantations. The next two anchors are fused together. If you take the time to look, you can find dozens of anchors hidden in the vast expanse of

Cane Bay. Further down, the sand funnel narrows and empties you out onto an immense wall at 100 feet. This is one of the top spots along the wall.

Divers should swim out 20 or 30 feet from the wall for an incredible panoramic view. Huge plate corals cascade from high above, never diminishing in size until they thin out way below. The wall itself forms a vast cove in which divers lose themselves and experience a sense of wonder as they are dwarfed by nature.

11. West Palm Beach (35'-130'; novice to expert): Located off a beautiful beach that once had a plethora of palm trees (hence the name) before a hurricane destroyed them, West Palm Beach offers a typically excellent St. Croix wall dive. There's lots of marine life, including many sponges, hard coral, and a wide variety of small and large fish.

12. Northstar (25'-130'; novice to expert): One mile west of Cane Bay, the wall reaches one of its steepest dropoffs. A vertical drop with a razor clean edge plummets downward from a 20-foot tabletop. This is one of the more common locations for shark and dolphin sightings. At 60 feet, a small sand shelf marks the entrance to a small cave, which is too low and shallow to enter, but has the potential for hiding creatures. Embedded upside-down in the wall above the cave is a large old anchor, while another one lies on the shelf itself.

The wall takes forms a sequence of huge coves, each about 100 yards wide. Outsized coral ribs separate the coves and provide landmarks divers use to help measure distance when navigating. Two awesome formations occur at extreme limits (below the limits of sport diving). Divers willing and able to go to the 130'-limit can observe these formations from above. Both have large pinnacles and one, called "The Abyss," is marked with an immense groove scored into the purely vertical wall.

Back up at the top edge of the wall, life is serene. Lovely coral formations, picturesque ridges, and bowl-like depressions make viewing comfortable for shallow diving and snorkeling.

13. Butler Bay Wrecks (45'-110'; novice – shallower wrecks – to expert): This dive site near Frederiksted features four wrecks that were intentionally sunk for diving. All are within about 100' of one another.

The shallowest wreck is the *Northwind* at about 50'. This 75-foot tug boat was used in the film *Dreams of Gold*, which documented Mel Fisher's search for the *Atocha*. After the filming, it was sunk by Cruzan Divers and now features lots of marine life.

The 110-foot *Suffolk Mae* is a short swim away. Sitting in about 65' of water, this trawler originally was wrecked on St. Croix during a 1984 hurricane before it was gutted and sunk for use as an artificial reef. The huge schools of horse-eye jacks are the highlight of this wreck.

At a depth of about 70', the 300-foot *Virgin Islander* serves as the largest and newest wreck at this site. Sunk in 1991, the barge is most notable for its sheer size.

Finally, the *Rosaomaira* is reserved for more advanced divers at 60' to 110'. This 177-foot Venezuelan freighter was sunk in 1986 and is packed with colorful marine life.

14. Frederiksted Pier (0'-30'; novice to expert): This is one of the Caribbean's most beautiful dives during the day or night. The quantity and quality of marine life is phenomenal, relative to the convenience of this dive. Don't miss a pier dive when you visit St. Croix.

St. John/St. Thomas

Since many of the dive sites around St. John and St. Thomas can be reached from either island and by many operators, they are grouped together below.

Though the on-shore life of St. John and St. Thomas is quite different, the underwater experiences are similar. If an operator on one of the islands doesn't offer a certain dive, another operator or the other island will.

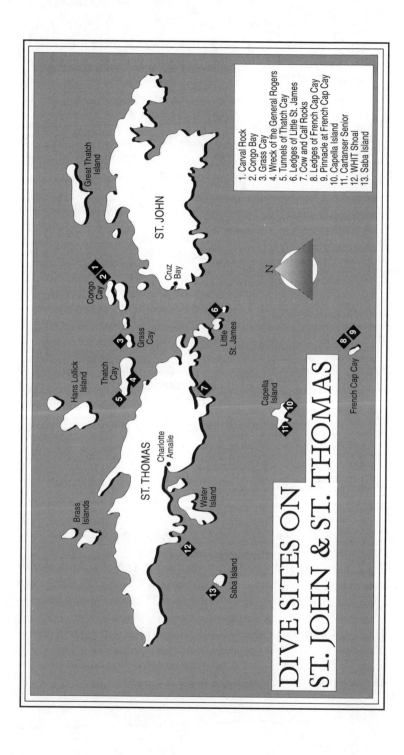

DIVE SITES ON
ST. JOHN & ST. THOMAS

1. Carval Rock
2. Congo Bay
3. Grass Cay
4. Wreck of the General Rogers
5. Tunnels of Thatch Cay
6. Ledges of Little St. James
7. Cow and Calf Rocks
8. Ledges of French Cap Cay
9. Pinnacle at French Cap Cay
10. Capella Island
11. Cartanser Senior
12. WHIT Shoal
13. Saba Island

N

ST. JOHN

Great Thatch
Island

Cruz
Bay

Congo Cay

Grass
Cay

Thatch
Cay

Little
St. James

Hans Lollick
Island

Capella
Island

French Cap Cay

Brass
Islands

ST. THOMAS

Charlotte
Amalie

Water
Island

Saba Island

Several operators also offer full-day dive trips to the wreck of the *Rhone* (see chapter on the BVI). If you're not visiting the BVI, you can plan a dive trip to *HMS Rhone* from either St. Thomas or St. John.

1. Carval Rock (20'-80'; advanced to expert): this rock is between St. John and St. Thomas, jutting through the water's surface. The currents through this site can make it a difficult or impossible dive. However, good conditions mean great diving. Divers can circle the island or plan an out and back dive, depending on the conditions and recommendations of the dive boat operator. Underwater, you'll find lots of marine life, ranging from stunning soft coral to large ocean-going fish. The rock formations in this area are fascinating.

2. Congo Cay (25'-130'; novice to expert): This is a very similar dive to Carval Rock, but conditions are typically a bit better. The rock formations provide hiding places for a wide variety of marine life, including lobsters.

3. Grass Cay (20'-60'; novice to expert): One of the most popular dives in the USVI, Grass Cay features superior conditions and easy diving. From huge sea fans to pretty coral formations, Grass Cay is an excellent introducory dive to St. John and St. Thomas' underwater world.

4. Wreck of the *General Rogers* (40'-65'; advanced to expert): Located just offshore from the Stouffer Grand Beach Resort, the wreck of the *General Rogers* is a USVI diving highlight. Since this 120-foot Coast Guard ship was intentionally sunk in 1972, it has had time to mature into a lively dive site. The ship is intact and is packed with coral and sponges, providing a cornucopia of color. The current through the wreck also makes for a healthy mix of fish.

5. Tunnels of Thatch Cay (20'-50'; intermediate to expert): This is a favorite dive for operators from both islands. It is typical underwater tunnel terrain and is considered one of the best dive sites in the USVI. There are more than a half-dozen distinct tunnels or arches at this site, with several short options and one that is nearly 60 feet in length. These swim-throughs feature lots of fish to accompany divers and plenty of coral on the walls.

6. Ledges of Little St. James (15'-50'; novice to expert): This dive, named for the island and the numerous ledges, features a large number of overhangs that are packed with coral life. The depth and high visibility of this site make it an ideal and popular night dive.

7. Cow and Calf Rocks (20'-40'; intermediate to expert): Located off southeast St. Thomas, the two largest rocks that break the surface supposedly look like humpback whales (a cow and her calf). You may need a vivid imagination to recognize the similarity! The site features plenty of caves, tunnels, arches, and ledges for detailed exploration. They are all alive with coral and fish, making for an interesting and relatively easy dive.

8. Ledges of French Cap Cay (40'-80'; intermediate to expert): Just off the southern shore of St. Thomas and Charlotte Amalie, this is another ledge dive. Great visibility and a large number of ledges, varying in size, shape, and marine life, make this dive a popular site. Many of the ledges are big enough to fit several divers and one even has a hole in the ceiling for divers to swim up and out.

9. Pinnacle at French Cap Cay (45'-100'; intermediate to expert): The boat ride to this large pinnacle is a bit longer than most USVI outings, but it can be well worth it. It starts in about 45 feet of water and can usually be seen from the surface. Be sure to take a photo of the two large outcroppings at the top.

10. Capella Island (30'-80'; novice to expert): The southern end of this island is a convenient dive for St. Thomas operators. The reef is alive and well, even though it was heavily damaged by Hurricane Hugo in 1989. The sloping landscape features lots of colorful coral and darting angelfish.

11. *Cartanser Senior* (20'-50'; novice to expert): This wreck of a 190-foot freighter is now divided into three wide open sections. The conditions make it ideal for an easy wreck dive and the daily fish feeding is an added attraction.

12. *WIT Shoal* (30'-90'; intermediate to expert): Situated southwest of St. Thomas's airport, this 300-foot ship is one of the finer artificial reefs around. It has five decks to explore and a colorful marine life that is swept in by the often fierce currents. On a good day, USVI diving doesn't get much better than this.

13. Saba Island (20'-50'; intermediate to expert): Located southwest of Charlotte Amalie, Saba Island's reef on the southeast side is similar to that off Capella Island. Look for the large arch at this site, as well as the rocky hideouts for lots of small critters.

Accommodations

Accommodation options in the USVI are as varied and plentiful as life below the water's surface. Though certain resorts do cater to divers and many of these are highlighted below, you may choose to stay at a hotel that doesn't specialize in hosting divers. The options listed below provide a general cost idea for travelers based on the following rates.

> Inexpensive: less than $100
> Moderate: $100 to $200
> Expensive: more than $200

These prices are for an average in-season standard double room for two and do not include any diving, dining, or other package options. Prices can drop dramatically with package deals and during the off-season from May to November. It's always best to check with the establishment directly for rates, special dive deals and availability.

St. Croix

Anchor Inn of St. Croix
58 King St., Christiansted
St. Croix, VI 00820
773-4000 or (800) 524-2030 (reservations)
FAX 773-4408

Comments: This downtown Christiansted waterfront hotel is a dive travel mecca. Located right on the harbor, the Anchor Inn is the ideal base for divers, thanks to Dive St. Croix and the Aqua-Lounge Club. Dive St. Croix (see "Dive Operators") features an Anchor Inn "Scuba Diving Package" and is located on the boardwalk right in front of the hotel. The Aqua-Lounge

Club (see "Entertainment"), an absolute must for every under-water enthusiast, is located on the second floor.

Rooms feature TVs, refrigerators, and small porches. Pico Bello and Antoines (see "Dining") offer excellent dinners. If you want to stay in Christiansted, this is a great choice. Moderate.

> **The Buccaneer Hotel**
> Box 25200
> Gallows Bay, Christiansted
> St. Croix, VI 00824
> 773-2100 or (800) 223-1108 (reservations)
> FAX 778-8215

Comments: One of the finest resorts in the Caribbean, this legendary pink hotel has almost everything. The large grounds feature a golf course, tennis, a spa, shopping, and much more. The spacious rooms and cottages are all close to the beach, pools, and restaurants. Steve Strauss provides complete diving services at the watersports center and the hotel offers dive packages.

The Buccaneer has been owned and operated by manager Elizabeth Armstrong's family since her grandparents opened the doors in 1947. Repeat guests indicate their success. This is a highly-recommended St. Croix resort. Moderate to Expensive.

> **Carambola Beach Resort**
> Box 3031, Kingshill
> St. Croix, VI 00851
> 778-3800; FAX 778-1682

Comments: This resort, crushed by Hurricane Hugo, has been completely renovated and has surpassed its former elegance. The bright red-roofed villas feature great views of the sea or the manicured gardens, mahogany furnishings, and pleasant patios. The large resort grounds and beach are perfect for a complete getaway. Expensive.

> **Hotel Caravelle**
> 44A Queen Cross St., Christiansted
> St. Croix, VI 00820
> 773-0687 or (800) 524-0410 (reservations)
> FAX 778-7004

Comments: The Hotel Caravelle has operated since its opening in 1967. Architecture, value, location, room size, and an experienced staff have made the Caravelle the success it is today. It has enjoyed a 90% occupancy rate for many years, which is one of the highest rates in the Caribbean. Elsie Galloway, the assistant manager, has been with Caravellel for 20 years and will make sure guests enjoy their stay.

Located right on the Christiansted waterfront, the pretty pink European-style hotel blends old world charm with modern amenities. The rooms are spacious and newly furnished, with a nearby freshwater swimming pool and sun deck overlooking the harbor. You can watch colorful sailboats glide by as you enjoy breakfast, lunch, or dinner at the award-winning Banana Bay Club (see "Dining").

Hotel Caravelle offers packages with nearby V.I. Divers and their 35' dive boat leaves directly from the hotel each morning. It's an ideal situation for divers staying in Christiansted. Moderate.

Chenay Bay Beach Resort
Box 24600, Christiansted
St. Croix, VI 00824
773-2918 or (800) 548-4457 (reservations)
FAX 773-2918

Comments: This resort is perfect for families. Ask about their all-inclusive packages, which can offer great deals. Moderate.

Club St. Croix Beach & Tennis Resort
3280 Golden Rock, Christiansted
St. Croix, VI 00820
773-4800 or (800) 635-1533 (reservations)
FAX 773-4805

Comments: This renovated property offers studio, one- , and two-bedroom apartments, with kitchens, decks, and great views of nearby Christiansted and Buck Island Reef National Monument. Moderate.

Colony Cove
3221 Golden Rock, Christiansted
St. Croix, VI 00820
778-1965 or (800) 828-0746 (reservations)
FAX 773-5397

Comments: These completely refurbished apartments are a great choice for families or couples. The owner, Susan Ivey, makes this a very special place. Moderate to Expensive.

Cormorant Beach Club
4126 La Grande Princesse, Christiansted
St. Croix, VI 00820
778-8920 or (800) 548-4460 (reservations)
FAX 778-9218

Comments: This well-situated north shore resort is a tropical oasis. If you want Caribbean elegance, this is the place to go. Expensive.

Frederiksted Hotel
5002 Gallows Bay, Christiansted
St. Croix, VI 00820
778-7670 or (800) 524-2025 (reservations)
FAX 778-4009

Comments: This hotel in town is one of the best deals in the USVI. It's convenient, clean, airy, and friendly. Inexpensive.

Hibiscus Beach Hotel
4131 La Grande Princess, Christiansted
St. Croix, VI 00820
773-4042 or (800) 442-0121 (reservations)
FAX 773-7668

Comments: The less-expensive sister hotel of the Cormorant Beach Club, the Hibiscus is a good deal for a beach hotel. Though all rooms offer nice ocean views, those in the Hibiscus building are the best. Inexpensive to Moderate.

Hilty House Inn
#2 Herman Hill, Box 26077
Gallows Bay, Christiansted
St. Croix, VI 00824
773-2594; FAX 773-2594

Comments: If you want an inn- or B&B-style experience on St. Croix, stay at the Hilty House. There are five guest rooms, an efficiency cottage, a big pool and quiet gardens. Located along the north shore. Hugh and Jacqueline Hoare-Ward make a stay here a unique Caribbean experience. Inexpensive.

> **Island Villas**
> 14A Caravelle Arcade, Christiansted
> St. Croix, VI 00820
> 773-8821 or (800) 626-4512 (reservations)
> FAX 773-8823

Comments: This company represents a wide selection of private homes throughout the island, which are ideal for longer stays and offer lots of flexibility. Moderate to Expensive.

> **King Christian Hotel**
> 59 King's Wharf, Christiansted
> St. Croix, VI 00820
> 773-2285 or (800) 524-2012 (reservations)
> FAX 773-9411

Comments: This in-town hotel is an ideal Christiansted choice for divers. The Sperber brothers run Dive St. Croix nearby (see "Dive Operators") and work in conjunction with the King Christian to produce reasonably-priced dive/accommodation packages. Inexpensive to Moderate.

> **Pink Fancy Hotel**
> 27 Prince St., Christiansted
> St. Croix, VI 00820
> 773-8460 or (800) 524-2045 (reservations)
> FAX 773-6448

Comments: This quiet Christiansted hotel is ideal if you want a typical Caribbean in-town hotel. The pretty pink facade leads to clean rooms and a nice courtyard pool. Inexpensive.

> **The Prince Street Inn**
> 402 Prince Street, Frederiksted
> St. Croix, VI 00840
> 772-9550 or (800) 771-9850

Comments: The Prince Street Inn offers charming and afford-able lodging and is situated just a five-minute walk from Cruzan Divers (see "Dive Operators").

Innkeepers Charlotte and Paul Pyles make this a special St. Croix spot, right in the heart of historic Frederiksted. In the 1800s, the inn served as a Danish Lutheran parsonage. It has been transformed into a six-room inn, with each room being unique in design and named for an old St. Croix estate. Favor-ites include Sweet Bottom (two bedrooms), Wood Cottage, and Whim, but any room at the Prince Street Inn is sure to become a favorite choice for guests.

> **St. Croix by the Sea**
> Estate St. John, Box 248, Christiansted
> St. Croix, VI 00821-0248
> 778-8600 or (800) 524-5006 (reservations)
> FAX 773-8002

Comments: Though this North Shore property doesn't have a natural beach, the views are spectacular. There is a man-made beach by the pool and the atmosphere is casual and relaxing. Moderate.

> **Sugar Beach Condominiums**
> 3245 Estate Golden Rock
> St. Croix, VI 00820
> 773-5345 or (800) 524-2049 (reservations)
> FAX 773-1359

Comments: These apartments range in size from studios to three-bedroom spreads and all of them have kitchens, patios or balconies, and great views. Sugar Beach is just a few minutes outside of Christiansted. Moderate to Expensive.

> **Villa Madeleine**
> PO Box 3109, Christiansted
> St. Croix, VI 00822
> 778-7377 or (800) 548-4461 (reservations)
> FAX 773-7518

Comments: This hilltop hotel is one of the most unusual places to stay in the Caribbean. The design and furnishings are exquisite, with more than 40 villas spread throughout the awe-inspiring property. Expensive.

Waves at Cane Bay
Box 1749, Kingshill
St. Croix, VI 00851-1749
778-1805 or (800) 545-0603 (reservations)
FAX 778-4945

Comments: This seaside inn just may be the perfect diver base on St. Croix. Kevin and Suzanne Ryan are the hospitable owners and innkeepers. Kevin says, "Words and pictures could never successfully convey the essence of what we offer our guests. St. Croix is one of the Caribbean's truly underated and unknown dive destinations."

The Waves at Cane Bay is the center point of about five miles of shoreline, hugging a dropoff wall that is largely accessible from shore. The Waves at Cane Bay doesn't run dive boats, but supports the shore diving market. Many of their guests opt for an occasional boat dive (with Anchor Dive Center, four miles away at Salt River), but the shore diving here is the main draw.

Though they take diving seriously, The Waves at Cane Bay is far from a typical dedicated dive hotel. Their client base is an eclectic mix of honeymooners, snowbirds, families, and divers who are looking for a vacation where they will get intimate with the Caribbean Sea. Their typical diving guest wants to make diving part of a vacation, but not necessarily the dominating part.

Each airy studio is equipped with a king-size or two twin beds and features a large screened balcony directly overlooking the Caribbean. Every room has color cable TV and kitchen facilities. Along with the dive operation, other amenities include a grotto saltwater pool, a half-mile stretch of beach just a short walk away, and there are many nearby island activities.

Kevin, Suzanne, Suzanne's sister Debbie, and her husband, Mitch Clark, are the main reasons that dive travelers love The Waves at Cane Bay. Personal service and attention, along with great shore diving, make this a wonderful choice on St. Croix.

St. John

Caneel Bay
PO Box 720
St. John, VI 00831
776-6111 or (800) 928-8889 (reservations)
FAX 693-8280

Comments: This is the mother of elegant resorts in the Caribbean. Founded way back in 1955 by Laurence Rockefeller, Caneel Bay provides the stay of a lifetime. The legacy of Mr. Rockefeller and his love of all things natural lives on at Caneel Bay. Located in the heart of the 5,000-acre Virgin Islands National Park, the resort is made up of seven separate beaches and is a naturalist's wonderland.

Caneel Bay's 171 guest cottages and rooms are spacious, featuring rich Caribbean woods, handwoven fabrics, and simple elegant furnishings. All rooms and cottages have spectacular views of one or more of Caneel Bay's seven beaches or beautiful gardens.

A good selection of outdoor activities accompanies the on-site dive shop, Paradise Watersports. The snorkeling at Caneel Bay is world-famous. Surface intervals are spent in the lap of understated luxury.

Caneel Bay's sister resort, Little Dix Bay, is just across the water in Virgin Gorda. If you want a truly special dive vacation, combine stays at both of these resorts with a few nights on one of their sailing ships. Expensive.

Cinnamon Bay Campground
PO Box 720, Cruz Bay
St. John, VI 00831
776-6330 or (800) 223-7637
FAX 776-6458

Comments: This classic Caribbean campground is a great place to stay when you're "roughing it" in St. John. The large National Park Service property features bare sites, tents, and cottages for rent. The bare tent sites provide one of the best accommodations deals in the Caribbean (around $15 per site), while the large floored tents and cottages run around $75 (still a bargain).

The well-run campground is an unusual and enjoyable St. John experience. Inexpensive.

> **Caribbean Villas and Resorts**
> Box 458, Cruz Bay
> St. John, VI 00831
> 776-5152 or (800) 338-0987
> FAX 779-4044

Comments: This efficient company offers more than 50 different homes on St. John. The accommodations, views, and service are typically first class. Moderate to Expensive.

> **Cruz Inn**
> PO Box 350, Cruz Bay
> St. John, VI 00831
> 776-6378 or (800) 221-1637 (reservations)

Comments: If you're looking for an inexpensive place to stay with a local flair, call the Cruz Inn. This simple guest house is located just two blocks from the Cruz Bay dock and has a variety of accommodations options. Inexpensive.

> **Gallows Point Suite Resort**
> PO Box 58
> St. John, VI 00831
> 776-6434 or (800) 323-7229
> FAX 776-6520

Comments: Highly recommended by Low Key Watersports, Gallows Point offers guests a fully-furnished harbor-view garden condominium, with a sunken living room, spacious bedroom, and larger-than-average bathroom. The resort is a five-minute walk from Low Key Watersports and the rest of Cruz Bay. Located on the water, the views of Pillsbury Sound or Cruz Bay are spectacular. Other amenities include freshwater swimming pool and fully-equipped kitchens. Expensive.

Harmony
PO Box 310, Cruz Bay
St. John, VI 00831
776-6226 or (800) 392-9004 (reservations)
FAX 776-6504

Comments: Harmony was planned and constructed by eco-tourism visionary, Stanley Selengut. Selengut developed Maho Bay Campground, a popular alternative Caribbean destination (see below) that has been a favorite ecotravel destintaion to many for years.

Stanley Selengut's new vision, Harmony, builds on the success of the campground just next door. State-of-the-art construction techniques, including low-impact building methods and the extensive use of recycled materials, such as plastic bottles, crushed glass, newsprint, old tires, and scrap lumber, were used in the development of Harmony.

Selengut loves to show guests dramatic examples of a resort that has minimal impact on the environment – a floor tile made entirely from the glass waste at a lightbulb factory or a square of carpet made of recycled plastic ketchup bottles and milk containers. Guests even slept on sheets made from organic cotton processed without dyes or bleaches.

A stay at Harmony is to be at one with nature (and St. John). His next venture, Estate Concordia, offers more nature (and a bit more comfort). Moderate.

Hyatt Regency St. John
Great Cruz Bay
St. John, VI 00830
693-8000 or (800) 233-1234 (reservations)
FAX 693-8888

Comments: This special resort has everything you would expect in a Caribbean Hyatt. Start with a pristine beach, add 285 rooms, suites, and townhomes, and place them all in a beautifully-landscaped tropical setting, and you have the Hyatt Regency St. John.

The resort offers an array of amenities and packages, including popular dive deals with Cruz Bay Watersports. Expensive.

Inn at Tamarind Court
PO Box 350, Cruz Bay
St. John, VI 00831
776-6378 or (800) 221-1637

Comments: This is another lower-priced St. John option right in Cruz Bay. The simple tropical rooms and decor give this guest house a local flavor. The popular restaurant is a bonus. Inexpensive.

Maho Bay Camps
PO Box 310, Cruz Bay
St. John, VI 00830
776-6240 or (800) 392-9004 (reservations)
FAX 776-6504

Comments: Like Cinnamon Bay Campground (see above), Maho Bay is a great place to stay if you're traveling on a budget in St. John. The attractive property is owned by Stanley Selengut, the famed eco-developer of Harmony (see above).

His campground, built in the 1970s and set in a tropical forest overlooking the beautiful beach and sea, is a rustic resort community of tent-cabins. More than 100 simple wood-frame structures made of canvas walls and roofs of plastic sheeting are spread throughout the property.

The simple cabins feature twin beds, basic furniture, a small kitchen area, and cooking utensils. The campground offers communal bath houses, a restaurant, social center, commissary, access to many hiking trails, an abundance of wildlife, a wide expanse of beach, and crystal-clear waters for snorkeling. The price (and experience) are right for thousands of visitors annually.

The campground is well run and provides an enjoyable St. John experience. Inexpensive.

Raintree Inn
PO Box 566, Cruz Bay
St. John, VI 00831
693-8590
FAX 693-8590

Comments: This centrally-located Cruz Bay inn is another budget choice. Raintree features several efficiency apartments and guest rooms, as well as the popular Fish Trap restaurant next door. Inexpensive.

Serendip
PO Box 273, Cruz Bay
St. John, VI 00830
776-6646
FAX 776-6646

Comments: Great views and bargains await guests (many of them repeat visitors) to this St. John secret. Fully-equipped one-bedroom and studio apartments offer quiet getaways and super sunsets here. Inexpensive to Moderate.

St. John Hostel
Bordeaux Mountain
St. John, VI 00830
693-5544
FAX 693-5544

Comments: The elevation is high and the prices are low at this Caribbean hostel. You get a bed and sheets for less than $25. Set high on Bordeaux Mountain, the hostel is close to some of the best hiking trails. Inexpensive.

Still Waters Guest Cottage
PO Box 716
St. John, VI 00831
693-8999 or (800) 835-7718

Comments: This new 1,300-square-foot home comes highly recommended by Low Key Watersports. It is set on a mountainside just five minutes from Cruz Bay. The deck, located on the first of two levels, offers spectacular views of Chocolate Hole, Hart Bay, and romantic Caribbean sunsets. You'll find an outdoor whirlpool tub to soothe tired muscles after a day of diving. There is also a fully-equipped kitchen. Expensive.

Virgin Grand Villas
6222 Estate Nazareth, Suite 8
St. Thomas, VI 00802
693-8856 or (800) 524-2038 (ext. 25) (reservations)
FAX 775-4202

Comments: It is located across the street from the Hyatt Regency and villa guests enjoy all of the Hyatt amenities while staying in large one- , two- , and three-bedroom townhomes. The diving with Cruz Bay Watersports make this an ideal villa choice. Expensive.

St. Thomas

Admiral's Inn
PO Box 6162, Veteran's Drive Station
St. Thomas, VI 00803-6162
774-1376 or (800) 544-0493 (reservations)
FAX 774-8010

Comments: Recommended and served by Sea Trade (Sea Horse Dive Boats/Dive Shop), the Admiral's Inn is a relaxing waterfront hotel set on four peaceful acres at the west entrance to the harbor of Charlotte Amalie. Large air-conditioned rooms feature verandas with magnificent views. There is a natural saltwater pool with a sandy beach area. Two restaurants serve three meals daily. The owners say, "You're near to town, but all you hear is the wind in the palms and your view is the blue sea." Inexpensive.

Blackbeard's Castle
PO Box 6041
St. Thomas, VI 00804
776-1234 or (800) 344-5771 (reservations)
FAX 776-4321

Comments: This is one of St. Thomas' most famous historic sites. It was built in 1679 as a watchtower to scan the Caribbean for pirates and enemy ships. The infamous Blackbeard is purported to have used the site as a lookout and hideaway. Since then, it has operated as a plantation, private estate, and a hotel.

The present owner, Brazilian-born Henrique Konzen, bought it in 1978 and, after extensive renovation, opened its doors to the public in 1985. It is a designated National Historic Landmark.

Overlooking Charlotte Amalie, the hotel offers one of the finest views in the USVI. The spacious guest rooms are quiet and intimate. There's a large pool overlooking the city. Beaches and shopping are just moments away, making this an ideal base for the historic-minded diver. Moderate.

> **Bluebeard's Castle Hotel**
> PO Box 7480, Charlotte Amalie
> St. Thomas, VI 00801-7480
> 774-1600 or (800) 524-6599 (reservations)
> FAX 774-5134

Comments: This modern red-roofed hotel offers great views and good service. Overlooking Charlotte Amalie, this is a solid in-town choice. Moderate.

> **Bolongo Club Everything Resort**
> 50 Estate Bolongo
> St. Thomas, VI 00802
> 779-2844 or (800) 524-4746 (reservations)
> FAX 775-3208

Comments: Owned and operated by the Doumeng family – Dick and Joyce Doumeng, their sons, daughter, and in-laws. Guests at Bolongo properties are treated like family. Their famous Club Everything Regular Plan includes airport transportation, inter-resort transportation, baggage handling, tennis, a fitness center, a kid's center, game rooms, theme nights, nightly entertainment, and watersports galore. Their All-Inclusive Plan covers all meals, drinks, tips, and taxes.

Located on the south shore, Club Everything includes 200 beachfront rooms and suites. There are two beaches, two swimming pools, and six tennis courts plus four different restaurants. The two beach locations allow the resort to retain an intimate feeling.

Bolongo is served by the St. Thomas Diving Club. An excellent choice for serious divers. Expensive.

Bolongo Elysian Beach Resort
50 Estate Bolongo
St. Thomas, VI 00802
779-2844 or (800) 524-4746 (reservations)
FAX 775-3208

Comments: Owned and operated by the Doumeng family (see above), the east end Elysian offers a hillside oasis on Cowpet Bay. All amenities, including a quiet beach and nice restaurant, are featured at this resort. It offers the same diving services through the St. Thomas Diving Club, making the resort an excellent choice for serious divers. Expensive.

Best Western Emerald Beach Resort
8070 Lindberg Bay
St. Thomas, VI 00802
777-8800 or (800) 233-4936 (reservations)
FAX 776-3426

Comments: Located near the airport (you'll get used to the intermittent noise), this is a convenient resort choice. The modern tropical hotel and its amenities offer a relatively good deal. Moderate to Expensive.

Grand Palazzo Hotel
6900 Great Bay Estate Nazareth
St. Thomas, VI 00802
775-3333 or (800) 545-0509 (reservations)
FAX 775-4444

Comments: The Grand Palazzo is definitely grand. The unique blend of warm Caribbean hospitality and striking renaissance architecture along with the excellent service make this one of the Caribbean's most elegant resorts.

Nestled in a 15-acre oceanfront estate along Great Bay on the east end and overlooking St. John, the Grand Palazzo features almost every amenity imaginable. It has 152 spacious junior suites, deluxe rooms, and one-bedroom suites. Each has a stunning oceanfront view from a private balcony or terrace. The dining at the resort matches the elegant setting.

The dive programs and packages, administered on-site by Arnaldo Fallcoff, are among the most personalized in the USVI.

The "Dive Into Paradise" package combines the beauty of the underwater world with the elegance of a Venetian palace. Expensive.

> **Hotel 1829**
> PO Box 1567
> St. Thomas, VI 00804
> 776-1829 or (800) 524-2002
> FAX 776-4313

Comments: If you want an historic stay right in the heart of Charlotte Amalie, this is the place. This small inn is popular with government workers and business people with duties in the capital. There is a wide choice of rooms and, consequently, prices. Inexpensive to Moderate.

> **Island View Guest House**
> PO Box 1903
> St. Thomas, VI 00803
> 774-4270 or (800) 524-2023 (reservations)
> FAX 774-6167

Comments: Recommended and served by Sea Trade (Sea Horse Dive Boats/Dive Shop), Island View is a relaxing 15-room guest house located midway between the airport and Charlotte Amalie. It is perched 545 feet above and overlooking the harbor. Each room has spectacular harbor views, but the six newer rooms offer the best spots. There is a freshwater pool. It offers excellent value. Inexpensive to Moderate.

> **Mafaolie Hotel**
> PO Box 1506
> St. Thomas, VI 00804
> 774-2790 or (800) 225-7035
> FAX 774-4091

Comments: Recommended and served by Sea Trade (Sea Horse Dive Boats/Dive Shop), this quaint property is a local favorite for the view, the food, and the company. The view of Charlotte Amalie is phenomenal and they say the hotel is conveniently "10 minutes from everything." Inexpensive to Moderate.

Marriott's Frenchman's Reef Beach Resort
PO Box 7100
St. Thomas, VI 00801
776-8500 or (800) 524-2000 (reservations)
FAX (800) 776-3054

Comments: Located just east of Charlotte Amalie, this large full-service resort has it all. The views from most of the tower rooms are spectacular, while the activities outside keep guests busy. Except for dive trips and Charlotte Amalie visits, you'll never have to leave the resort. Expensive.

Marriott's Morning Star Beach Resort
PO Box 7100
St. Thomas, VI 00801
776-8500 or (800) 232-2425 (reservations)
FAX 774-6249

Comments: Situated right next to the Frenchman's Reef, this Marriott property features quieter, bungalow-style rooms. on the beach. Expensive.

Pavilions & Pools
Route 6
St. Thomas, VI 00802
775-6400 or (800) 524-2001
FAX 775-6110 (ext. 251)

Comments: This unique hotel offers a pool and deck for each tropical room, which also has a full kitchen. Diving excursions are available with Dive In at Sapphire Beach next door. Expensive.

Point Pleasant Resort
6600 Estate Smith Bay #4
St. Thomas, VI 00802
775-7200 or (800) 524-2300 (reservations)
FAX 776-5694

Comments: Point Pleasant is complete Caribbean pleasure. Located on a steep hill full of tropical foliage, the resort offers wonderful views and a wide range of accommodations. This is a truly Caribbean resort and a complete get-away-from-it-all spot. The Chris Sawyer Dive Center is located down the hill at the Stouffer Renaissance Grand Beach Resort. Expensive.

Ramada Yacht Haven Hotel & Marina
5400 Long Bay Rd., Charlotte Amalie
St. Thomas, VI 00802
774-9700 or (800) 228-9898 (reservations)
FAX 776-3410

Comments: This pink Charlotte Amalie sailing spot is a perfect choice for water lovers staying in town. The busy property and accompanying facilities offer decent rooms and prices to match. Moderate.

Sapphire Beach Resort & Marina
PO Box 8088
St. Thomas, VI 00802
775-6100 or (800) 524-2090 (reservations)
FAX 775-4024

Comments: Located right on one of the island's best beaches, Sapphire Beach offers relatively quiet accommodations with full kitchens. Each of the suites and villas faces the Caribbean and has a private balcony and a living/dining room. The sparkling white beach is one of the best features. Dive In is on-site and offers a selection of packages through the resort. Expensive.

Secret Harbour Beach Resort
Box 7576
St. Thomas, VI 00801
775-6550 or (800) 524-2250 (reservations)
FAX 775-1501

Comments: This sparkling white resort sits right on pretty Nazareth Bay. The accommodations offered include studios and suites. Expensive.

Stouffer Grand Beach Resort
PO Box 5267, Smith Bay Road
St. Thomas, VI 00801
775-1510 or (800) 233-4935 (reservations)
FAX 775-2185

Comments: One of the Caribbean's early premier resorts, you can't go wrong with the Stouffer Grand Beach. This popular place has everything for everyone, including a Chris Sawyer Dive Center. Package deals are available. Expensive.

Sugar Bay Plantation Resort
6500 East Smith Bay
St. Thomas, VI 00802
777-7100 or (800) 927-7100
FAX 777-7200

Comments: Sugar Bay is definitely a sweet place to stay. The huge white resort features large rooms, most of which have great views and all of which have balconies. It's a busy and popular choice. Expensive.

Dining

Like a USVI vacation, dining can be anything you want it to be. You will find almost every cuisine and atmosphere imaginable.

Dining in the USVI is not cheap. The restaurants listed below are rated according to the following scale.

Inexpensive: less than $15 per person
Moderate: between $15 and $30 per person
Expensive: more than $30 per person

St. Croix

Christiansted

Antoine's, 58 King St., 773-0263. Located on the boardwalk right at the Anchor Inn, this friendly place offers Continental cuisine. The 10-page menu features a huge variety of fresh and imported seafood.

Chart House, Kings Wharf, 773-7718. Some of the best seafood, accompanied by great views. Moderate to Expensive.

Club Comanche, Strand St., 773-2665. This is a casual and eclectic choice, with tall peacock chairs and a tropical terrace setting. Moderate.

Harvey's, 11 Company St., 773-3433. If you want local cooking in a casual atmosphere, this is the place to go. Sarah serves as your chef and hostess. Inexpensive.

Kendricks, Queen Cross St., 773-9199. One of the top restaurants on the island, with excellent service and well-prepared Continental cuisine. Expensive.

Pangaea, 2203 Queen Cross St., 773-7743. This restaurant features a wide array of Caribbean and other cuisines. The decor and menu are sure to please everyone. Moderate.

Pico Bello, 58 King St., 773-2663. Located inside the Anchor Inn, this casual restaurant offers a wide array of authentic Italian food, with a menu that changes daily.

Top Hat, 52 Company St., 773-2346. This popular spot, frequented by locals and repeat visitors, features Danish cuisine and is run by a friendly Danish couple. Moderate to Expensive.

Frederiksted

Blue Moon, 17 Strand St., 772-2222. The decor, food, and music are all pleasantly jazzy. This is a great place for cocktails, dining, entertainment, and watching the sun set.

Elsewhere on St. Croix

Café Madeleine, Route 82 (outside Christiansted), 778-7377. One of the island's most elegant restaurants and locations (at Villa Madeleine, see "Accommodations"), this eatery serves innovative cuisine. Expensive.

Duggan's Reef, Teague Bay, 773-9800. This beachfront East End spot is popular with locals looking for a cold drink and some hearty food.

Villa Morales, Estate Whim (just off Route 70), 772-0556. This is another excellent family-run restaurant featuring local dishes and a relaxed atmosphere.

St. John

Cruz Bay

Ellington's, Gallows Point Suite Resort, 776-7166. On the grounds of a well-located resort (see "Accommodations"), this restaurant offers some of the best views and seafood on the island. Moderate to Expensive.

The Fish Trap, Raintree Inn, 776-9817. Set amidst lots of tropical trees, the seafood is quite justifiably the highlight of dining here. Moderate.

Lime Inn, Downtown, 776-6425. This local joint features friendly service and several specialty nights. Moderate.

Pusser's, Wharfside Village, 774-5489. Part of the popular Pusser's chain, this British-style pub is a great place to meet fellow travelers from around the world. Moderate.

Etta's, Inn at Tamarind Court, 776-6378. This is the best bet for local color and cooking in Cruz Bay. It's also a great place to stay (see "Accommodations"). Inexpensive.

Elsewhere on St. John

Le Chateau de Bordeaux, Bordeaux Mountain on Route 10, 776-6611. Offering one of the finest dining experiences in the Caribbean, this French-influenced restaurant features wonderful views and one of the most creative menus. Expensive.

Don Carlos, Coral Bay, 776-6866. If you have a hankering for a Caribbean-influenced Mexican meal, head to this Coral Bay outpost. Inexpensive to Moderate.

Shipwreck Landing, 776-8640. While in Coral Bay, you may want to check out the drink specials and local seafood specialties at this popular spot. Inexpensive to Moderate.

Miss Lucy's, Friis Bay, 779-4404. If you want a truly local St. John dining experience, head to Miss Lucy's. It's easiest to reach in your own vehicle and the drive will be worth it, once you taste the food. Inexpensive.

St. Thomas

Charlotte Amalie

Blackbeard's Castle, Blackbeard's Castle, 776-1234. Located at the hotel by the same name (see "Accommodations), the views and Sunday brunch are rightfully popular.

Entre Nous, Bluebeard's Castle, 776-4050. This elegant restaurant is as popular with locals as it is with tourists. They all come for creative Continental cuisine and spectacular views of Charlotte Amalie and the harbor. Expensive.

Hotel 1829, Government Hill, 775-2810. This classic Caribbean hotel features an equally classy restaurant. Expensive.

Little Bopeep, Back St., 776-9292. If you manage to locate this unique restaurant, you'll find some of the best local cuisine in the USVI. Inexpensive.

Hard Rock Café, International Plaza, 775-5555. You know what to expect at this popular chain. Moderate.

Victor's New Hide-Out, Sub Base, 776-9379. If you're looking for local cooking in a French town setting, this is the perfect place. Inexpensive to Moderate.

Elsewhere on St. Thomas

Agave Terrace, Point Pleasant Resort, 775-4142. Even if you aren't staying at this wonderful resort, stop by for a drink or meal. Moderate to Expensive.

Eunice's Terrace, Smith Bay, 775-3975. Eunice's cooking is the star at this ever-popular St. Thomas restaurant. Inexpensive to Moderate.

For the Birds, Scott Beach, 775-6431. Located right on the beach, this casual eatery is quite popular for its Mexican meals and ribs. Moderate.

Piccola Marine Café, Red Hook, 775-6350. If you're heading to or from St. John and have a hunger for some good pizza and friendly company, check out this popular Red Hook hangout.

Entertainment

When it comes to entertainment, the nightlife on all three islands can be as tame or wild as you want it. On St. Croix, action can be found at several of the Christiansted and Frederiksted restaurants mentioned above. But if you really want to go where local and visiting divers relax, head to the **Aqua-Lounge Club** (773-0263) at the Anchor Inn Hotel (see above). Owner Tony Doos, who has several nice restaurants on the island, is a St. Croix diving enthusiast who loves sharing his underwater secrets. Further afield, check the schedule of the **Island Center for the Performing Arts** at 778-5272, or play a game of dominoes and share a beer with a pig at the **Mt. Pellier Domino Club** (772-9914, see "Sightseeing").

On sleepy St. John, the choices are a bit more limited. There are several nice bars and restaurants in Cruz Bay that offer entertainment and it's easy to find them by wandering around town. The major resorts also offer entertainment.

Over on St. Thomas, there are many more choices of after-dark activities. Along with the resorts, some popular entertainment spots include **Castaways**, 76-8410; **Club Z**, 776-4655; and **Sugar Bay Disco**, 777-7100.

Sightseeing

St. Croix

Several excursions around St. Croix should be planned. Like the diving, St. Croix's riches on land are still a secret. History, culture, and sheer beauty are bountiful on this island.

Guided tours are available with **St. Croix Transit**, 772-3333, and **St. Croix Tours**, 772-6700. These trips, running about $10 per hour, can serve as a great introduction to St. Croix. However, a rental car is the best bet if you plan to take a number of trips throughout the island. It's easy and flexible.

Christiansted

Visitor Center: Located in the Old Scale House right on the harbor. The friendly staff can provide information about Christiansted, Frederiksted, and the rest of the island. Have them point you to the Old Customs House directly across from their office.

Old Customs House: Though this building now contains offices for the important work of the National Park Service on St. Croix, it once housed the customs offices for this busy port city. The 1734 building is definitely worth a picture or two.

Post Office: You can mail your postcards at this 1749 building, which once housed the busy importing and exporting business of the Danish West India & Guinea Company.

Steeple Building: Located on Company Street, this one-time Danish church is now a National Park museum, with many exhibits about the history and culture of St. Croix. Admission, which also gets you into Fort Christiansvaern, is $2 for adults and free for children under 16 and senior citizens. It is generally open on weekends and Wednesdays from 9am to 4pm, 773-1460.

Christian "Shan" Hendricks Market: Also located on Company Street, this active local market is open on Wednesdays and Saturdays. It is well worth a visit.

Government House: Located on King Street near the harbor, this pretty Danish structure was built as a home in 1747. It served as Danish government offices and is now used as USVI government offices. Visitors can enter the courtyard and second-story ballroom free of charge.

Fort Christiansvaern: This bright yellow Danish-built fort is a National Historic Site. The 1749 structure once protected the harbor for the Danes, but it now just offers outstanding views and a good St. Croix history lesson.

Admission, which also gets you into the Steeple Building, is $2; children under 16 and senior citizens may visit free of charge. The fort is open on weekdays from 8am to 5pm, and 9am to 5pm on weekends and holidays (except Christmas Day), 773-1460.

Frederiksted

You should definitely stop to admire this quaint little town, though it can get a bit busy when a cruise ship is at the new pier.

Visitor Center: Located at the cruise ship pier, this office can provide information about the town, as well as anything you need to know about the rest of the island.

Fort Frederik: Though many Danish buildings burned during a devastating fire in 1878, this 1760 Danish fort remains as a symbol of the town's Danish heritage. There are several historic and art exhibits. Admission is free and the hours are 8:30am to 4:30pm on weekdays only, 772-2021.

Market Place: Located at the intersection of Market and Queen Streets, this little local market is active in the early morning almost every day. A great place to watch the locals as they trade goods and catch up on gossip.

St. Paul's Episcopal Church: Situated on King Cross Street, the town's major church was built in 1812.

St. Croix Aquarium: This small local facility offers an interesting overview of St. Croix sea life. The exhibits are well presented and the staff is friendly. Open on Fridays, Saturdays, and Sundays, 772-1345.

Elsewhere on St. Croix

There's lots to see on this island and it's generally easy to get around. Contrary to popular belief, you'll find most locals friendly and helpful.

Buck Island Reef National Monument: This site is well run by the National Park Service and is generally more interesting to non-diving snorkelers who enjoy the shallow reef and marked "sightseeing" snorkeling trail. Excursions out to the reef are popular and well organized.

Pt. Udall: This is the easternmost point in the U.S.

St. George Village Botanical Gardens: For plant lovers, these gardens offer a feast of greenery. Set in the ruins of a 19th-century sugar plantation, they display literally hundreds of plants and flowers. There is also an interesting exhibit profiling the various ecosystems on St. Croix, ranging from desert-like conditions to rain forest. Admission is $3 for adults and $1 for kids. The gardens are open from 10am to 3pm daily (except Sunday and Monday), 772-3874.

Estate Whim Plantation Museum: This old 19th-century sugar plantation and estate has been restored to its former glory. The house, historic exhibits, and grounds are an interesting side-trip for the whole family. Admission is $5 for adults and $1 for kids. Located just a few miles outside of Frederiksted, Estate Whim is open 10am to 4pm daily (except Sunday and Monday), 772-0598.

Sandy Point Beach: This beautiful beach is the home of huge leatherback turtles that arrive each spring (usually March to June) to lay their eggs in the sand. Earthwatch groups run interesting excursions at night to protect the eggs. For further information, contact the St. Croix Environmental Association at 773-1989.

Estate Mount Washington Plantation: This old sugar plantation offers a free walking tour of the grounds, the mill, and a rum factory. It's usually open every day, 772-1026.

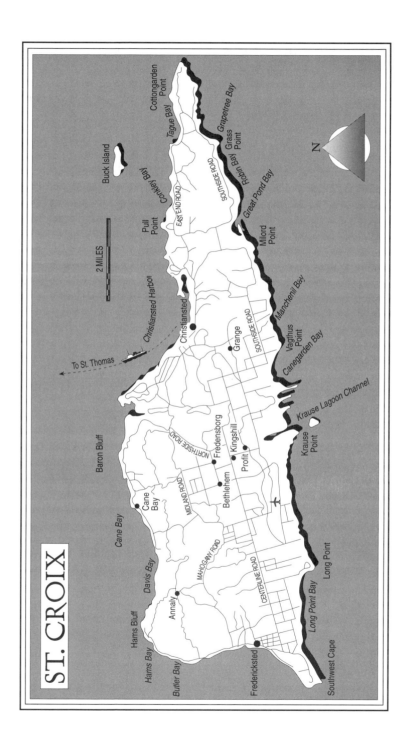

ST. CROIX

Cottongarden Point
Grapetree Bay
Tague Bay
Grass Point
SOUTHSIDE ROAD
Robin Bay
Great Pond Bay
Buck Island
Conkey Bay
Pull Point
EAST END ROAD
Milford Point
2 MILES
Christiansted Harbor
Manchenil Bay
Christiansted
Grange
Vagthus Point
SOUTHSIDE ROAD
Canegarden Bay
To St. Thomas
Krause Lagoon Channel
Baron Bluff
Fredensborg
Kingshill
Krause Point
NORTHSIDE ROAD
Profit
Cane Bay
Bethlehem
MIDLAND ROAD
Cane Bay
Davis Bay
Hams Bluff
MAHOGANY ROAD
Annaly
Long Point
Long Point Bay
CENTERLINE ROAD
Hams Bay
Butler Bay
Frederiksted
Southwest Cape

N

St. Croix Leap: This is surely one of the most interesting places above sea level in the Virgin Islands. The eclectic workshop for local artists features a large number of mahogany pieces. It's the perfect place for an unusual St. Croix souvenir and is usually open every day, 772-0421.

Mt. Pellier Domino Club: This bar and restaurant is home to what must be the world's most photographed pig. Back in the barn, Miss Piggy rose to fame for guzzling can after can of Old Milwaukee. Though she now drinks non-alcoholic beer because of failing health, it's still a sight to behold (and photograph). Be sure to linger for a cold drink, some great local food, or a look at the constant games of dominoes played by locals. The road down to the north shore is know as "The Beast," an incredibly steep hill used for the bike portion of the America's Paradise Triathlon. It eventually leads past the Carambola before heading to Cane Bay.

Cane Bay: The drive along the north coast is one of the Caribbean's finest routes. Cane Bay offers a nice beach and some of the best shore diving in the entire Caribbean. Even if you're not staying there, be sure to stop in and see Kevin and Suzanne Ryan. You should try to stay overnight if you like nice people, a relaxed atmosphere, and spectacular shore diving.

Salt River Marina: This little marina is the home of Anchor Dive Shop and famed "Sharkey" Vince (see "Diving"). Columbus landed on the beach nearby. The Salt River Landing National Historic Park and Ecological Preserve is an on-going project of exhibits and trails.

Judith's Fancy: This idyllic spot features the ruins of a 17th-century estate and great views of local homes and Salt River Bay, where Columbus landed.

St. John

St. John is easy to explore and can take a few hours or more than a week, depending on your interests. Many of the island's sightseeing adventures have been created by Mother Nature.

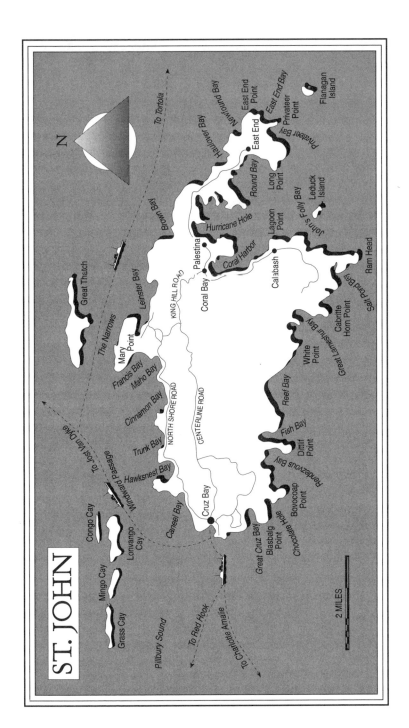

Although a rental car is still the best bet for sightseeing on St. John, there are several good tours. The taxis, which are typically open air medium-size buses, offer a wide variety of island tours. Rates run about $10 per hour, and you can probably join a cruise ship or other organized tour for less.

The National Park Visitor Center: 776-6201, provides a number of guided tours on and off the island for moderate fees. There are snorkel trips, coastal walks, birding trips, and the popular Reef Bay Hike, all with rangers that share their knowledge and experience with you. The rangers also offer many other programs.

Cruz Bay: St. John's capital may be the quintessential Caribbean town. Situated right on the stunning bay are the National Park Service Visitor Center (see above), shopping, dining, and watersports.

Caneel Bay: One of the Caribbean's most famous resorts, this posh establishment was developed by Laurence Rockefeller in the 1950s and has remained much the same since. It's a great place for a splurge, whether you're spending the week or just stopping for a meal or the great beach and snorkeling.

Christ of the Caribbean Statue: This famous statue was erected in 1953, but the view has always been there.

Trunk Bay: This is surely one of the most alluring beaches in the world. Stop for a spectacular picture of the beach, before you descend to the parking lot. This is a great place to relax in the sun when the cruise ship passengers haven't overtaken it for the day.

Cinnamon Bay: This attractive beach also features some great hiking and the Cinnamon Bay Campground (see "Accommodations") if you're traveling on a shoestring budget.

Maho Bay: This favorite Caribbean camping area now also features Harmony Resort (see "Accommodations"), one of the world's first and best ecologically-correct properties.

Annaberg Plantation: Almost every St. John tour includes a stop at these ruins. The 18th-century sugar plantation features an interesting self-guided walking tour and great views. It is administered by the National Park Service, 776-6201, and you may visit free of charge (they often offer interesting programs).

Coral Bay: This smaller sister town of Cruz Bay is one of the quietest small towns in the Caribbean. You'll find several local dining and accommodations options here (see "Dining" and "Accommodations").

East End: The quietest end of the island offers great views overlooking the meeting point of the Caribbean Sea and the Atlantic Ocean.

Lameshur Bay: The beach at Lameshur offers more of the island's great snorkeling.

Bordeaux Mountain: Route 10 leads across the island and offers some spectacular views, including the highest point at the top of Bordeaux Mountain (1,277 feet). There's also a popular restaurant here (see "Dining").

Reef Bay Trail: Though you can tackle this hike on your own, the National Park Service hike makes it much more enjoyable and easy. They drop you off at the trailhead and a ranger leads you to the bottom of the mountain, where a boat awaits to take you back to town (see above). It's well worth the $10 charge.

Enighed Estate Great House: Located just outside Cruz Bay, this interesting restored house is now home to the Elaine Ione Sprauve Library and Museum. Visitors find local artifacts and art, as well as friendly local staffmembers. It's open 9am to 1pm and 2pm to 5pm on weekdays, 776-6359.

St. Thomas

When you're not diving, dining, or enjoying the amenities of your chosen accommodations, St. Thomas has everything else imaginable, from beautiful beaches to one of the world's great shopping ports.

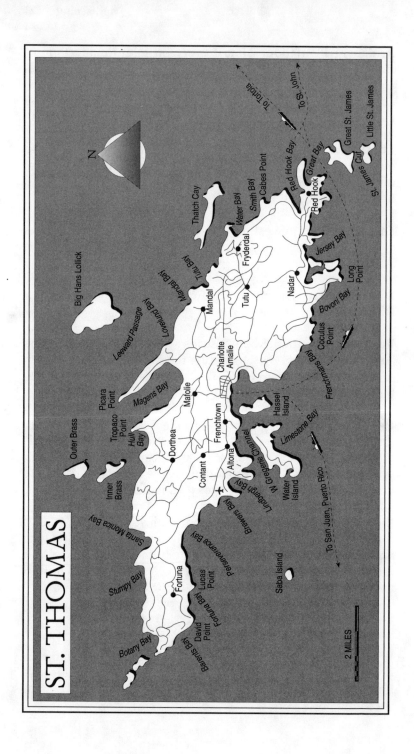

ST. THOMAS

To Tortola

To St. John

Great St. James

Little St. James

St. James Cut

Red Hook Bay

Great Bay

Red Hook

Cabes Point

Smith Bay

Water Bay

Thatch Cay

Jersey Bay

Fryderdal

Long Point

Mandal Bay

Tutu Bay

Mandal

Tutu

Nadar

Bovoni Bay

Big Hans Lollick

Leeward Passage

Loverundal Bay

Coculus Point

Charlotte Amalie

Frenchmans Bay

Picara Point

Magens Bay

Matolie

Hassel Island

Tropaco Point

Hull Bay

Dorthea

Frenchtown

Altona

Limestone Bay

Outer Brass

Inner Brass

Contant

W. Gregene Channel

Water Island

Lindbergh Bay

To San Juan, Puerto Rico

Santa Monica Bay

Brewers Bay

Saba Island

Stumpy Bay

Preservance Bay

Fortuna

Lucas Point

Fortuna Bay

David Point

Brewers Bay

Botany Bay

N

2 MILES

It all starts with Charlotte Amalie, where a centuries-old port is now dominated by the cruise ship scene. You can shop 'til you drop, but you can also explore an incredible amount of USVI history. Outside of St. Thomas, sandy beaches, blue water, and incredible views await sightseers.

Guided Tours: If you don't rent a car or want to get a local's perspective, St. Thomas has a broad selection of sightseeing tours. From island tours to sunset cruises, there are many great ways to see all the island has to offer.

For standard tours, expect to pay about $10 per hour, per person, which is typically negotiable. **Tropic Tours**, 774-1855 offers excellent half-day island and shopping tours, as well as full-day St. John excursions. **Virgin Islands Taxi Association** drivers, 774-4550, offer standard two-hour tours, but they can tailor a trip to suit your needs and budget. The drivers are typically friendly, and the smaller the tour, the better the experience.

For a really unusual view of the Virgin Islands, a "flightseeing" tour with **Seaborne Seaplane Adventures**, 777-4491, is highly recommended. Their 40-minute flight (about $80) covers St. Thomas, St. John, and some of the BVI. They have other tours available. The friendly owners also offer flightseeing tours in Alaska.

If you simply can't get enough of life below the surface or you're traveling with a non-diver, **Atlantis Submarine**, 776-5650, is an alternative way to travel underwater. Their touring submarine, located in Charlotte Amalie, holds about 50 people and carries passengers 150 feet down on a reef. The tour is ideal for non-divers and kids. It costs about $70 for adults and $25 to $35 for children. Atlantis Submarine trips have inspired many new divers.

One of the most popular tour boats on the island is *Kon Tiki*, 775-5055. Their three-hour afternoon tour includes lots of rum punch and people, music, and a stop at Honeymoon Beach on Water Island. It costs about $30 for adults and $15 for kids.

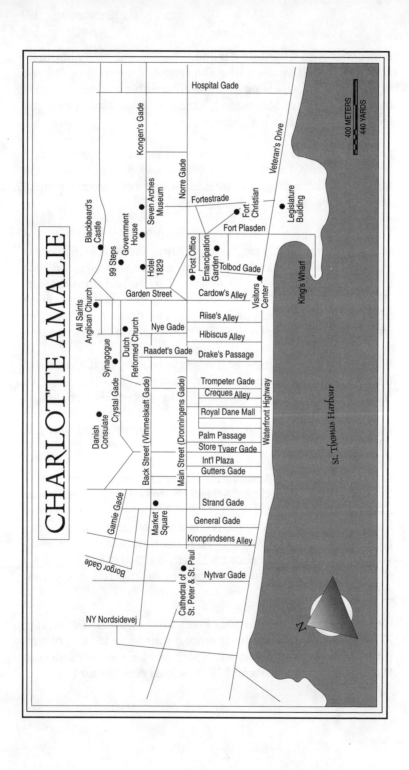

CHARLOTTE AMALIE

Hospital Gade

Kongen's Gade

Norre Gade

Veteran's Drive

Seven Arches Museum

Blackbeard's Castle

Government House

99 Steps

Hotel 1829

Fortestrade

Fort Christian

Fort Plasden

Legislature Building

Post Office

Emancipation Garden

Tolbod Gade

All Saints Anglican Church

Garden Street

Cardow's Alley

Visitors Center

King's Wharf

Nye Gade

Riise's Alley

Hibiscus Alley

Synagogue

Dutch Reformed Church

Raadet's Gade

Drake's Passage

Crystal Gade

Trompeter Gade

Creques Alley

Danish Consulate

Back Street (Vimmelskaft Gade)

Main Street (Dronningens Gade)

Royal Dane Mall

Palm Passage

Store Tvaer Gade

Int'l Plaza

Gutters Gade

Waterfront Highway

St. Thomas Harbour

Gamle Gade

Market Square

Strand Gade

General Gade

Kronprindsens Alley

Borgor Gade

Nytvar Gade

Cathedral of St. Peter & St. Paul

NY Nordsidevej

N

400 METERS
440 YARDS

Charlotte Amalie

Visitor Information Center: Located in Emancipation Square, this helpful visitor center is a great place to start a walking tour of Charlotte Amalie and get information about sightseeing throughout the island.

Emancipation Garden: This busy area is the heart of Charlotte Amalie and is a great place to get your bearings and people-watch.

Fort Christian: This national landmark was built during the 17th century and is the island's oldest building. It has been used for many things over the years and several of the dungeon rooms are now used for a museum of USVI history. It is open on weekdays from 8:30am to 4:30pm, Saturdays from 9:30am to 4pm, and Sundays from noon to 4pm, 776-4566. Admission is free.

Legislature Building: The USVI Senate meets in this green building.

Cruise Ship Port and Havensight Mall: Located about a half-mile east of the city center, this busy cruise ship port also features lots of shopping and dining for cruise ship passengers who don't want to make the trek into the heart of Charlotte Amalie. On busy days, there may be more than six ships in port.

Post Office: You can send your postcards from this busy city post office, but you should also take a look at the murals painted by Stephen Dohanos, a *Saturday Evening Post* artist.

Hotel 1829: This is a classic Caribbean hotel (see "Accommodations") and well worth a quick look inside, a drink at the bar, an excellent meal, or a room for one or more historic nights.

99 Steps: Though there are more than 99 steps, a walk up this staircase is a walk up one of the city's oldest "streets."

Government House: This is the official residence of the governor of the USVI. The first floor's exhibits and murals are open to the public, while a second floor visit must be arranged by calling 774-0001. The second floor includes several small paintings by Camille Pissarro, who was born in Charlotte Amalie.

Seven Arches Museum: This quiet 19th-century home has been restored and offers a view of early times on the island. The house is private, but tours (about $5) of the interior are offered every day, except Monday, from 10am-3pm. Call 774-9295.

Blackbeard's Castle: Offering one of the best views in St. Thomas, this hotel offers a great spot to stop for a drink, a meal, a sunset, or the night (see "Accommodations" and "Dining"). The tower is said to have been utilized by the pirate Edward Teach.

All Saints Anglican Church: This eye-catching church was built in 1848 to commemorate the end of slavery in the Virgin Islands.

Dutch Reformed Church: This cream-colored church was built in 1744 and then rebuilt in 1844 after a fire.

Synagogue of Beracha Veshalom Vegmiluth Hasidim (Congregation of Blessing, Peace, and Loving Deeds): If you only visit one place in Charlotte Amalie, make it this synagogue. Located at 15 Crystal Gade, it opened in 1833 and is the second oldest synagogue in the Western Hemisphere (Curacao's is the oldest) and the oldest synagogue building in continuous use under the American flag. The sand floor and dark mahogany of the interior are a dramatic sight.

Danish Consulate: Bjerge Gade turns into stairs leading to the landmark Danish Consulate. The red-and-white flag and high view make for fine pictures.

Market Square: If you like the flavor of local markets, this is a great place to wander. You'll find vendors of all types, from fresh exotic fruits and vegetables to local herbs and spices.

Cathedral of St. Peter and St. Paul: Located along Main St. (Dronningens Gade), this attractive pink parish church was built in 1848 and features wonderful murals inside.

Frenchtown: Located about a half-mile west of the center of Charlotte Amalie, this colorful harbor village retains an old West Indian feel. You'll find lots of tiny houses and streets, as well as quite a few good local restaurants (see "Dining"). The walk along the harbor on Waterfront Highway is always interesting.

Elsewhere on St. Thomas

Red Hook: The winding road east out of Charlotte Amalie leads past many beautiful resorts and vistas, finally reaching the booming hamlet of Red Hook, which serves as the main ferry dock for St. John. Some shopping and dining have also sprouted here.

Coki Beach and Coral World: This busy little beach is great for a quick swim or snorkel tour. There are lockers (which should be used, if needed) and lots of vendors offering everything from food to fins. Coral World, 775-1555, is located at one end of the beach. Though it may not fascinate seasoned divers, it does offer the largest reef tank in the world, many aquariums, other exhibits, and a knowledgeable staff. You'll also find an underwater mailbox where you can mail postcards home. Expect to pay about $15 for adults and $10 for children. The Seaworld Explorer Semi-submarine also offers reef tours for $12 to $20. Coral World's hours are 9am to 6pm daily.

Tillet's Gardens: Providing a wonderful contrast to shopping in Charlotte Amalie, this local artists' gallery features a wide variety of work, including the colorful silk-screens of the namesake Tillet. The maps are particularly popular. There is also a restaurant and bar in the cool courtyard area.

Estate St. Peter Greathouse Botanical Gardens: If you're looking for an unusual way to spend a couple of hours outdoors, this is a great choice. Situated on the edge of a mountain, the gardens offer a nature trail with hundred of tropical trees, plants, and colorful flowers. Inside the greathouse, you'll find the work of local artists. The friendly staff members make this a wonderful excursion. Admission is free and it's open daily 9am to 5pm, 774-4999.

Drake's Seat: This famous overlook is the spot from which Sir Francis Drake watched ship's movements in the area. To the east are the BVI and Drake's Passage, with a pretty view of Magens Bay (one of the most appealing beaches in the entire Caribbean) and Mahogany Run as well. The best time to visit for pictures and peace is in the late afternoon or early evening.

Mountain Top: This establishment claims to have invented the banana daiquiri, but they've definitely inherited a great view.

Hull Bay: If you want to see more local life, stop by this fishing village, where you'll find friendly locals, primitive campsites, and good music on Sundays.

Brewer's Beach: This beach is popular with students from the University of the Virgin Islands nearby and is across the street from the Reichhold Center for the Arts, 774-8475, a large amphitheater offering a busy calendar of events.

Other Activities

One of the many beauties of a USVI dive vacation is the variety of things to pursue when you're not diving or sightseeing.

Beaches

Simply sunning and swimming at a beautiful beach is the most popular pastime. On St. Croix, some of the best beaches include Buck Island, Cane Bay, and several beaches along the West End. On St. John, Caneel Bay, Cinnamon Bay, Hawksnest Bay, and Trunk Bay are only a few of the best beaches. Over on St. Thomas, try Bluebeard's Beach, Bolongo Bay, Coki Beach, Hull Bay, Limetree Beach, Magens Bay, Morningstar Beach, and Sapphire Beach.

Boating

The beautiful blue Caribbean Sea plays host to a large number of boats and it's easy for vacationers to rent one for an hour or a week. Along with the live-aboard options mentioned above, many charter companies will arrange a boating vacation. Some of the best contacts include **Annapolis Sailing School**, (800) 638-9192; **Avery's Boathouse**, 776-0113; **Caribbean Adventures**, (800) 626-4517; **Caribbean Sailing Charters**, (800) 824-1331; **Caribbean Yacht Charters**, (800) 225-2520; **Caribbean Yacht Owners Association**, (800) 944-2962; **Club Nautico**, 779-2555; **Island Yachts**, (800) 524-2019; **Nauti Nymph**, 775-5066; **Ocean Incentive**, (800) 344-5762; **Ocean Runn**, 693-8809; **Proper Yacht Charters**, 776-6256; **See and Ski**, 775-6265; and **VIP Yacht Charters**, (800) 524-2015.

Day-trip boating possibilities for St. Croix (mostly to Buck Island) include **Big Beard's Adventure Tours**, 773-4482; **Llewellyn's Charter**, 773-9027; **Mile Mark Watersports**, 773-2628 or (800) 524-2012; and **Teroro II**, 773-3161.

In St. John, try **Alcyone**, 776-6922; **Bob Nose**, 776-6922; **Breath**, 779-4994; **Camrita**, 776-6922; **Destiny**, 776-6922; **Motor Yacht Cinnamon Bay**, 776-6462; **Restless**, 776-6922; **Spree**, 771-3734; and **Stampede**, 693-8000.

On St. Thomas, contact **Alexander Hamilton**, 775-6500; **Bright Star**, 775-8277; **Coconut**, 775-5959; **Daydreamer**, 775-2584; **Franya**, 690-7900; **Halcyon Days**, 775-7211; **Independence**, 775-6547; **Kon Tiki**, 775-5055; **Moonshadow**, 775-6072; **Morningstar**, 775-1111; **My Way**, 776-7751; **New Horizons**, 775-1171; **Nightwind**, 775-4110; **Pirate's Penny**, 775-7990; **Rendezvous**, 779-2357; **Stormy Petrel**, 775-7990; **Sundance**, 778-9650; **Wild Thing**, 774-8277; and **Winifred**, 775-7898.

Fishing

On St. Croix, contact **Cruzan Divers** at 772-3701, **MileMark** at 773-2628, or **Ruffian Enterprises** at 773-6011. On St. John, contact **Gone Ketchin'** at 776-7709 or one of the St. Thomas outfitters. On St. Thomas, contact **American Yacht Harbor** at 775-6454, the **St. Thomas Sportfishing Center** at 775-7990, or one of many fishing boats at Red Hook's marina.

Golf

St. Croix offers several golf possibilities. **The Buccaneer**, 773-2100, features a spectacular seaside setting for golf alongside a wonderful resort. **The Carambola**, 773-8844, has a Robert Trent Jones course. **The Reef Club**, 773-8844, features a less formal nine-hole course. On St. Thomas, **Mahogany Run** provides another glorious setting. Designed by Tom and George Fazio, this stunning course has beautiful views and challenging holes. Contact the club at 775-5000.

Horseback Riding

The rolling hills and rain forest of St. Croix are ideal for the equestrian set. Contact **Paul and Jill's Equestrian Stables** at 772-2880 for a spectacular ride suited to your tastes and abilities.

To see the natural beauty of St. John by saddle, call **Pony Express Riding Stables** at 776-6494. On St. Thomas, call **Rosenthal Riding Ring** at 775-2636.

Parasailing

If you want to admire the USVI from above, try parasailing. Many resorts on St. Croix and St. John offer the opportunity. On St. Thomas, check at your resort or contact **Caribbean Watersports** at 775-4206.

Shopping

Shopping until you drop can be a major activity here. The great prices and duty-free status have made the USVI a shopping haven.

On St. Croix, Christiansted offers the most variety. The best bets are on and around **Company and King Streets**, as well as the **Caravelle Arcade** and the **Pan Am Pavillion**. The shopping in Frederiksted is quiet and more local. Don't forget to head to **St. Croix Leap**, which is surely one of the most interesting places above sea level in the Virgin Islands. This eclectic workshop for local artists features a wide variety of mahogany pieces. It's the perfect place for an unusual St. Croix souvenir and is usually open every day, but call 772-0421 to check their hours.

Sleepy St. John has some great little stores, creating a much more subdued shopping experience compared to St. Thomas. **Cruz**

Bay features a number of quaint stores, as well as a wide selection of shops at **Mongoose Junction** and **Wharfside Village** in Cruz Bay. The National Park headquarters in Cruz Bay also offers a great selection of books.

St. Thomas is a Caribbean shopping mecca and Charlotte Amalie is its capital. The options include local art, jewelry, china, linens, liquor, and much more. The hundreds of shops along **Waterfront, Main, and Back Streets** are packed with merchandise. Other possibilities include the cute alleys in between the major streets, **Vendors Plaza**, and **Havensight Mall** out at the cruise ship dock. Further afield, **Tillet's Gardens**, 775-1405, offers a selection of local art.

Snorkeling

As you would expect, great diving means great snorkeling. The USVI offers a number of excellent snorkeling sites.

Some of the best ones include **Buck Island** on St. Croix; **Caneel Bay, Haulover Bay, Hawksnest Bay, Leinster Bay**, and **Trunk Bay** on St. John; and **Coki Beach, Hull Bay, Long Point, Magens Bay**, and **Smith Bay** on St. Thomas.

Tennis

All three islands cater to tennis enthusiasts. Most of the tennis courts are located at resorts, but they often let non-guests play for a fee.

Windsurfing

Windsurfing is quite popular on all three islands, with most major resorts on St. John and St. Thomas offering lessons and rentals. On St. Croix, there are two popular operators: **Tradewindsurfing** at 773-7060 and **Virgin Territory Surf and Sail** at 773-4810.

Additional Reading
from Hunter Publishing

ADVENTURE GUIDE TO THE HIGH SOUTHWEST
$14.95, ISBN 1-55650-633-3, 384pp

> " ... a conscientious and beautifully written guide...."
> *Reviewer's Bookwatch*

Hiking, mountaineering, trail riding, cycling, camping, river running, ski touring, wilderness trips – a guide to enjoying the natural attractions of the Four Corners area of Northwest New Mexico, Southwest Colorado, Southern Utah, Northern Arizona, and the Navajo Nation and Hopiland. Includes all practical details on transportation, services, where to eat, where to stay and travel tips on how to cope with the harsh terrain and climate. The most adventurous guide to this region on the market. Maps.

> "Each title in this fine series shares a similar format: extensive background on history, economics, and politics, flora and fauna, and culture and religion; the daily practicalities of life; what to see and do." *Library Journal*

Among others in the **Adventure Guide** series:

OREGON & WASHINGTON *$13.95, ISBN 1-55650-709-7, 224 pp*
BAHAMAS *$12.95, ISBN 1-55650-705-4, 224pp*
BERMUDA *$12.95, ISBN 1-55650-706-2, 192pp*
CATSKILLS & ADIRONDACKS *$9.95, ISBN 1-55650-681-3, 170pp*
COSTA RICA 2nd Ed. *$15.95, ISBN 1-55650-598-1, 470pp*
PUERTO RICO 2nd Ed. *$14.95, ISBN 1-55650-628-7, 304pp*
CANADA *$15.95, ISBN 1-55650-315-6, 320pp*
VIRGIN ISLANDS 3rd Ed. *$14.95, ISBN 1-55650-597-3, 280pp*
EVERGLADES & THE FLORIDA KEYS
  $14.95, ISBN 1-55650-494-2, 192pp
BAJA CALIFORNIA *$11.95, 1-55650-590-6, 280pp*
BELIZE 3rd Ed. *$14.95, ISBN 1-55650-647-3, 288pp*
DOMINICAN REPUBLIC 2nd Ed. *$14.95, 1-55650-629-5, 270pp*
THE ALASKA HIGHWAY *$15.95, 1-55650-457-8, 228pp*
COASTAL ALASKA & THE INSIDE PASSAGE
  $14.95, ISBN 1-55650-583-3, 288pp

THE CARIBBEAN - A WALKING AND HIKING GUIDE 2nd Ed.
By Leonard M. Adkins
$12.95, ISBN 1-55650-708-9, 320pp

> " ... Offers what no other guide provides information on en-
> joying the Caribbean exclusively on foot. Easy walks and
> rugged hikes are profiled. Keep this if you already own it;
> otherwise, try to purchase it from a used book dealer."
> *Library Journal* on the 1st Edition, now out of print.

This spectacular book covers the Caribbean in depth, offering
walks for adventurous travellers and families alike. From sightseeing walks of the major towns to strenuous overnight hiking in the
rainforest of Dominica this book has it all. Each hike is rated for
difficulty. Maps, black and white photos, contact numbers.

HAWAII - A WALKER'S GUIDE 2nd Ed.
By Rod Smith
$12.95, ISBN 1-55650-694-5, 184pp

Packed with unforgettable adventures in Kauai, Maui, Oahu,
Molokai, Lanai and Hawaii. A practical guide to the most scenic
walks to suit all travellers, from easy strolls of a few hours to
multi-day excursions. Maps and black and white photos.

COASTAL CALIFORNIA - A CAMPING GUIDE
By George Cagala
$11.95, ISBN 1-55650-679-1, 272pp

This no-nonsense guidebook is the only source you will need as
you travel along the spectacular coastal strip of California. As the
shoreline stretches for more than 1,200 miles, the author tells you
where you can bivouac in a motor home beneath a grove of 250-foot
redwoods, rent a teepee on an island a few miles off the mainland
or a cabin on a tiny peninsula of stubborn rock. Maps, fees, black
and white photos, regulations, supplies, amenities, telephone numbers, reservations, how to get there and much more.